TARTS
SWEET AND SAVOURY

TARTS
SWEET AND SAVOURY

MAXINE CLARK
PHOTOGRAPHY BY MARTIN BRIGDALE

RYLAND
PETERS
& SMALL

LONDON NEW YORK

Dedicated to my sister Jacks, my friend, who is known to make a decent tart or two, and is a constant source of inspiration.

First published in Great Britain in 2003
by Ryland Peters & Small
Kirkman House,
12–14 Whitfield Street
London W1T 2RP
www.rylandpeters.com

10 9 8 7 6 5 4 3 2

Printed in China

ISBN 1 84172 419 X

A CIP record for this book is available from the British Library.

Senior Designer Steve Painter
Commissioning Editor Elsa Petersen-Schepelern
Editor Kim Davies
Production Meryl Silbert
Art Director Gabriella Le Grazie
Publishing Director Alison Starling

Food Stylists Maxine Clark, Linda Tubby
Stylist Helen Trent
Indexer Hilary Bird

Author's acknowledgements

Thanks to all those listed below for helping to create this beautiful book.

Elsa, for asking me to do this book and being a kindly dragon where necessary.

Kim, for her good-humoured and efficient editing.

Steve for his elegant design and calm control during photography – and his great taste in tarts!

Martin for his luscious, light, atmospheric photography and his relish for a good tart!

Helen for her simply spectacular styling and boundless enthusiasm.

And Becca Hetherston, without whose good-humoured assistance in all things tarty at the studio, I could not have managed.

Notes

All spoon measurements are level unless otherwise specified.

All eggs are medium, unless otherwise specified. Uncooked or partly cooked eggs should not be served to the very young, the very old, those with compromised immune systems, or to pregnant women.

Before baking, weigh or measure all ingredients exactly and prepare baking tins or sheets.

Ovens should be preheated to the specified temperature. Recipes in this book were tested in several kinds of oven – all work slightly differently. I recommend using an oven thermometer and consulting the maker's handbook for special instructions.

contents

home is where the tart is ...

I just love making tarts, and have done so ever since watching my grandmother baking us little tarts when we came home from school, and letting us fill them with lemon curd. But then it's in the genes, you see: I come from a family of bakers and I am Scottish (we love to bake). Making your own pastry well is one of the simple pleasures in life. Your own pastry bears no resemblance to the bought stuff in either taste or texture, AND you can monitor the ingredients. Ready-to-roll pastry made with real butter is almost impossible to find in Britain, and I will not accept hydrogenated vegetable fat as an ingredient for pastry. It produces pastry with no flavour and a colourless appearance. Whatever fat you use, it must be pure, and your flour good quality. Good ingredients make great dishes!

Tarts are faster and much less complicated to make than pies, as they are not covered. They can be rustled up at a moment's notice, even if you haven't made the pastry already (try to make batches and divide into useful amounts to thaw later). Don't be scared to make your own pastry – with modern appliances such as the food processor, bad pastry is a thing of the past. Don't be put off buying ready-made pastry if it encourages you to become a tart-maker!

The majority of tarts in this book are sweet – it naturally worked out that way – but there are recipes for everyday tarts, tarts for a special occasion, classic tarts and comfortingly self-indulgent tarts. People notice when they bite into a homemade crust, revealing a heavenly interior, so get to grips with pastry-making and you'll never look back. Like baking your own bread, it is a very satisfying and rewarding experience. Go ahead and tackle a tart today!

basics

equipment and utensils

For pastry-making

A large **work surface** (a marble slab if you are lucky, but make sure it is big enough) is essential for making a tart. Never roll out pastry in a cramped area or you will risk rolling unevenly or stretching the pastry. The surface should be cool (not next to the stove) to prevent the pastry becoming soft and unmanageable.

Accurate **weighing scales** to get the quantities and proportions correct.

Measuring spoons for accurate measuring, necessary with all baking. Recipes in this book require all measurements to be level.

Large and small heatproof **measuring jugs**. They are dual purpose – for accurate measuring of liquid ingredients, and suitability for the microwave (which I use as a kitchen tool like all other equipment).

Fine and medium **sieves** are essential for sifting all flour to aerate it and remove any lumps, thus contributing to a lighter pastry. Icing sugar should ALWAYS be sifted in a fine sieve – the lumps will never beat out.

Assorted **mixing bowls** – I find I use light plastic bowls or wide stainless steel ones for pastry-making, but glass or Pyrex are perfectly suitable. The important thing is to make sure the bowl is big enough for the job – you want plenty of room to move for your hands and the ingredients when rubbing in. This, too, aerates the pastry.

A **food processor** is a MUST if you have hot hands, or if you think you can't make pastry! It removes all the fear of butter melting into the flour, because it mixes fat and flour so quickly and evenly. Just remember to pulse the machine when adding liquids so that the dough will not be overworked and become tough.

A **flour sifter/shaker** is not absolutely necessary, but it does stop you adding too much extra flour to the work surface or pastry. Too much extra flour destroys the proportions and affects taste and texture.

Several **pastry brushes** so you always have a dry one to hand for brushing excess flour off pastry, and one for brushing liquids and glazes.

A **pastry scraper** for scraping the dough off a work surface, and for cleaning off all the messy bits. Indispensable.

A **palette knife** can be used instead, but is best used for chopping in the flour in French pastries such as pâte brisée (page 29).

Microplane graters were a revelation to me, and once acquired, you'll wonder how you ever lived without them. There are three grades – fine, medium and coarse. Fine is perfect for grating lemons, nutmeg, garlic and ginger and Parmesan. Medium for other cheeses, and general grating. Coarse is perfect for grating butter into pastry or grating streusel pastry (page 115).

A **pastry blender** is something I have used only occasionally, but some cooks swear by it. It is a series of thin metal loops connected to a handle, which you use to cut the fat into the flour. It prevents 'hot hand syndrome' and aerates the pastry. I prefer an old round-bladed cutlery knife (or two – one in each hand) to cut in the fat.

All-purpose **clingfilm or plastic bags** are absolutely necessary to wrap pastry before chilling or freezing, protecting it and preventing it from drying out.

Always keep a bottle of **iced water** in the refrigerator so you have chilled water to hand for pastry-making.

Choosing tart tins

Good solid **baking sheets** that won't buckle in the oven are ESSENTIAL – really good ones cost a fortune, but they soon become part of the family!

A selection of sizes of **tart tins** with removable bases – the heavier the better, so they won't buckle. Heavy tins will cook the tart or pastry more evenly. It is worth spending extra money on a few very good tins rather than buying a lot of cheap ones that will warp. (I don't recommend china or glass dishes for baking pastry as they give the dreaded 'soggy bottom'.) Traditionally, fluted edges designated sweet fillings while plain edges indicated a savoury filling. The most useful sizes are 20.5, 23, 25 cm and sometimes a 30 cm for a crowd.

Some people prefer **flan rings** to set on a baking sheet, instead of the loose-based tins. These are the chef's choice as they are strong and easy to store. The most useful are 20.5, 23 and 25 cm.

A **tarte tatin pan** is a luxury, but worth having if this is your favourite tart! It is a heavy-based tin that is specially designed to conduct the heat well to caramelize the apples without burning them. Two sizes are useful – 20 and 28 cm.

Metal or enamel **pie plates** with a wide rim to take a good crust – both deep and shallow – are essential for American-style tarts and pies, and tarts that need a decorative edge such as treacle tart. Diameters from 20.5 to 23 cm.

Assorted **springform tins** are great for deeper tarts, as they are easy to remove once the tart is cooked. The most useful are 20.5, 23 and 25 cm.

Tartlet tins in various sizes and shapes. I collect these – although the most useful are loose-based and measure 9–10 cm for individual tarts and 6–7 cm for tartlets.

Patty pans/tins are the traditional tins for making little tartlets in bulk, like curd or jam tarts.

Mini muffin tins are wonderful for making cocktail-sized tartlets in bulk and little filo tartlets.

Yorkshire pudding tins (4-hole) make larger individual shallow tarts in bulk, and fit into the oven nicely.

Rolling out and lining the tin

Ruler – a must for checking tin sizes and drawing or cutting straight edges when decorating pastry.

Long straight **rolling pin** (wooden or nylon) with no handles. I find that handles spoil the even rolling action of the pin. Always keep your rolling pin somewhere where the surface won't be damaged by other kitchen utensils (not in the utensil drawer!) If using a rolling pin to smash or pound, use the end, not the long surface that will become pitted and will transfer marks onto the pastry.

Sharp **cook's knife** or thin-bladed filleting knife for trimming – it must be razor-sharp to cut through the pastry and not drag it.

Large **serrated knife** for trimming and slicing – this stays nice and sharp and is good for cutting baked pastry shells.

A **fork** for pricking bases and decorating.

Assorted sizes of **palette knives** – I have three sizes, and I use all of them equally at different times. A large one will help to loosen rolled-out pastry from the work surface, a small one will lift little pastry circles into a tart tin, and a tiny one will lift pastry decorations onto the tart edge.

Clingfilm, greaseproof paper, kitchen foil, non-stick baking parchment, for wrapping pastry, lining tins and for baking blind (page 19). Note that baking parchment and greaseproof paper are completely different things; one is non-stick and the other just impervious to grease.

Ceramic or metal **baking beans** or just a jar of rice or dried beans which can be used over and over again for baking blind. I use all sorts of things to weigh down the pastry when baking blind. It depends on what's hanging around in the cupboard or on the size of the tart. Little tarts can be filled with rice or lentils, larger ones with dried beans, peas, pasta or a mixture.

Assorted **biscuit cutters**, both plain and fluted, to cut out small tarts to line tartlet tins, bun tins or mini muffin tins.

Decorating pastry

Biscuit cutters of all types. You can create dozens of decorative edges using leaf cutters, shaped cutters – even animals, to customize your tarts. I am forever adding to my collection.

Pastry wheels make short work of cutting straight lines and give decorative edges.

A **small sharp knife** will help to cut patterns on decorations.

A **lattice cutter** is a clever way of making a professional-looking lattice top for tarts and pies. It acts like a roller, cutting out a lattice, which can be opened up like a web to drape over a tart. It lacks the homemade look, however!

Baking and cooling tarts

An **electronic timer** is one of my most essential pieces of kit. You cannot possibly cook pastry and not burn it without one!

Oven gloves – a must, no damp tea towels to burn your hands!

Wire or metal **cooling racks** – assorted sizes, 1 large and 2 medium.

Mesh cloches/domes are very useful for protecting the tart against damage as it cools, letting the air circulate freely.

Large **slice** or **cake-lifter** will help to lift the tart onto a plate without it falling to bits.

Serrated palette knife is useful to slice the tart then serve it or lift onto a plate.

A word about microwaves

All microwaves differ in power output, so be guided by the maker's handbook. The times given here are only guidelines – you must get to know your own microwave.

A word about fan-assisted ovens

Most must usually be set 20 degrees lower than regular ovens. Consult the maker's handbook. This is important when baking.

Care of equipment

All metal tins should be gently washed in warm soapy water, rinsed and dried thoroughly (in the turned off oven after baking), or they will rust.

Some tins just need a wipe with kitchen paper – doing this will gradually build up a non-stick patina on the tin, making it look well-used and giving it character.

top tart tips

- Water/liquid quantities are never exact as there are so many variables. A rule of thumb is to add slightly less than is stated, as you can always add more – but too much and the dough is lost!

- Always have a dry pastry brush on hand to remove excess flour.

- If your hands are sticky with dough, stop everything and wash them, then dry them and dust with flour . This will stop the pastry sticking to them and prevent horrible dry flaky bits falling off your hands into the pastry when you roll it out!

- Try to flour your hands and the rolling pin rather than bathing the pastry in flour to prevent sticking.

- When rolling pastry, keep it moving on a 'hovercraft' of flour and it will never stick.

- Rolling pastry directly on a piece of non-stick baking parchment or clingfilm will mean it can be moved round easily and will not stick to the work surface!

- Always roll directly away from you and move the pastry round by short turns in one direction so that you roll it evenly.

- Setting two chopsticks (or similar) on either side of a dough before you roll it out will help you to roll it out evenly to the thickness of the chopstick and no less.

- If you are a beginner, don't try to roll out the pastry too thin – just cook it for a bit longer when you bake it blind (page 19).

- There is no need to grease a tin before lining. All pastry has fat in it and will in effect be non-stick – it is the filling leaking out over the edges or through holes that makes pastry stick.

- When you line a tart tin, try rolling the flour-dusted pastry around the rolling pin to help you to pick it up – this will avoid stretching the pastry and stop it shrinking when cooking.

- Use a small piece of extra pastry wrapped in a piece of clingfilm to help to push the pastry into the edges of the tin. Once this is done you can press the pastry up the sides of the tin and cut off the overhang with a very sharp knife. I like to press the pastry again into the flutes of the ring after cutting off the excess to give a good shape.

- If in doubt, CHILL-CHILL-CHILL! Raw pastry will benefit from thorough chilling at every stage – I like to freeze pastry-lined tins before baking blind as this really sets the pastry, so it holds its shape. Freeze the unbaked tart shell after lining the tin with pastry, even just for 15 minutes. This gives the pastry a good rest and makes the tart easy to line with foil and beans when baking blind. Work quickly, and get it into the oven before it thaws, and you will have a perfect pastry shell!

- ALWAYS chill a double crust pie before baking.

- Always glaze then chill a pie before making any marks on the pastry – it will be easier to do.

- Always chill a pie before making slits in the pastry.

- Always place a tart on a baking sheet before baking. This will make it easier to lift in and out of the oven and prevent any spillage burning on the bottom of the oven.

- If travelling with the tart, put it back into the ring to make carrying easier and safer, and wrap in a clean tea towel.

making pastry

basic shortcrust pastry

This is the classic method for making short and crumbly shortcrust pastry. It is made with half butter and half lard – the butter for colour and flavour, and the lard for shortness. If you have cool hands, the hand method is best because more air will be incorporated than if you use a food processor. If you have hot hands, the food processor is a blessing! The quantities of water added vary according to the humidity of the flour, so always add less than the recipe says – you can add more if the dough is dry, but once it is a sticky mess, your pastry could be a disaster!

250 g plain flour

a pinch of salt

50 g lard (or white cooking fat), chilled and diced

75 g unsalted butter, chilled and diced

2–3 tablespoons chilled water

makes about 400 g pastry, enough to line a tart tin, 23–25 cm diameter, or to make a double crust for a deep pie plate, 20–23 cm diameter

Note The quantities given here are generous. Any leftover pastry may be frozen or used to make small tartlets. It is not really worth making pastry in small batches – I often make double quantities, freezing one for later.

1 Sift the flour and salt together into a bowl. (Or sift into a food processor.)

2 Rub in the lard and butter until the mixture resembles breadcrumbs. (Or add to the food processor and blend for 30 seconds for the same result.)

3 Add the water, mixing lightly with a knife to bring the pastry together. (Or add to the food processor, and pulse for 10 seconds until the pastry forms large lumps. Add another tablespoon of water and repeat if necessary.)

4 Knead lightly on a floured work surface, then shape into a flattened ball, wrap in clingfilm and chill for at least 30 minutes before rolling out.

rich shortcrust pastry

This is a wonderfully light and crumbly pastry. It is made the same way as the Basic Shortcrust Pastry (page 12) but is enriched with egg and made with butter only. It is best used for richer pies and tarts, or where the shell is more than just a carrier for the filling and the taste of the pastry is important. It can be made in a food processor, following the method given for the Dill and Nutmeg Pastry (page 15), or the classic way, directly on the work surface. The processor method is quicker and easier, and there is no sticky mess to clear up. But the classic method gives a slightly lighter result – and besides, there is something satisfying about making pastry by hand.

250 g plain flour

½ teaspoon salt

125 g unsalted butter, chilled and diced

2 medium egg yolks

2 tablespoons iced water

makes about 400 g pastry, enough to line a tart tin, 23–25 cm diameter, or to make a double crust for a deep pie plate, 20–23 cm diameter

1 Sift the flour and salt together into a bowl, then rub in the butter.

Note For a Sweet Shortcrust Pastry, sift 2 tablespoons icing sugar with the flour and salt.

2 Mix the egg yolks with the 2 tablespoons iced water. Add to the flour, mixing together lightly with a knife.

Note The pastry must have some water in it or it will be too difficult to handle. If it is still too dry, add a little more water, sprinkling it over the flour mixture 1 tablespoon at a time.

3 Turn the mixture out onto a lightly floured work surface.

4 Knead lightly with your hands until smooth.

5 Form the dough into a rough ball.

6 Flatten slightly, then wrap in clingfilm and chill for at least 30 minutes before rolling out.

dill and nutmeg pastry (above)

250 g plain flour

a pinch of salt

1 teaspoon freshly grated nutmeg

4 tablespoons chopped fresh dill

125 g butter, chilled and diced

1 medium egg yolk

2–3 tablespoons iced water

Put the flour, salt, nutmeg and dill into a food processor, add the butter and blend until the mixture looks like fine breadcrumbs. Mix the egg yolk with the iced water and add to the machine. Blend again until it begins to form a ball – add another tablespoon of water if it is too dry and blend again. Tip out onto a floured work surface and knead lightly until smooth, then shape into a flattened ball. Wrap in clingfilm and chill for 30 minutes before rolling.

cheese shortcrust pastry

225 g plain flour

1 teaspoon salt

3 tablespoons freshly grated Parmesan

125 g unsalted butter

2 medium egg yolks

2–3 tablespoons iced water

To make the pastry, sift the flour and salt into a bowl. Stir in the Parmesan, then rub in the butter. Mix the egg yolks with 2 tablespoons iced water, then stir into the flour mixture to bind to a firm but malleable dough (add another tablespoon of water if it is too dry and blend again). Knead lightly until smooth then shape into a flattened ball. Wrap in clingfilm and chill for at least 30 minutes before rolling out.

american pie crust

This is a recipe for the classic American pie crust, given to me by a good friend from New York state. The quantity is enough for two pies – she makes and bakes one straight away and freezes the rest for another time. You could make and bake both pies now, freeze all the dough to use later, or make double quantity and freeze it all. To give the crust a richer flavour and delightful golden colour, unsalted butter can be substituted for the cooking fat, or you can use half butter and half cooking fat (or lard). It is a very light, crumbly pastry when baked – similar to shortcrust and very homely.

375 g plain flour

a good pinch of salt

250 g white cooking fat, chilled

1 medium egg, beaten

1 tablespoon wine vinegar or lemon juice

4 tablespoons iced water

makes about 675 g pastry, enough for 2 deep tart shells, 24 cm diameter

1 Sift the flour and salt into a large bowl.

2 Cut in the fat using 2 round-bladed knives or a pastry blender (or do this in a food processor).

3 Beat the egg in a separate bowl or jug.

4 Stir in the vinegar or lemon juice, then add the water.

5 Pour the wet mixture into the dry mixture, then cut it in with the knives or pastry blender again.

6 Bring the dough together quickly using your hands.

7 Knead until smooth either in the bowl or on a floured work surface.

Divide in 2 so it is easier to roll out later.

8 Shape the dough into a flattened ball, wrap in clingfilm, then chill for at least 30 minutes before rolling out.

Baking and freezing

Divide in 2. Roll out each piece to about 3 mm thick. Line both tart tins, prick all over with a fork and chill or freeze for 15 minutes. Line with foil or all-purpose clingfilm and fill with baking beans. For partial baking, bake at 200°C (400°F) Gas 6 for 10–12 minutes, or, for full baking, 15–18 minutes until just colouring around the edges. Remove the foil or clingfilm and beans (cool and and reserve the beans for another day), then return the tart shells to the oven to dry out for 4–5 minutes until golden.

For freezing, divide the uncooked dough in 2 and form into flattened balls ready to thaw and roll out.

rolling out, lining a tart tin and baking blind

The secret of a beautiful crisp tart shell lies in these crucial initial stages of making the pastry case. The pastry should be rolled out as thinly as you dare, lifted into the tin without being stretched, then gently eased in and trimmed. The uncooked case must be chilled or frozen before baking to combat shrinkage. Baking blind will ensure that the tart does not have a soggy base. Keep the baked base in the tin while the filled tart is cooking or it could collapse.

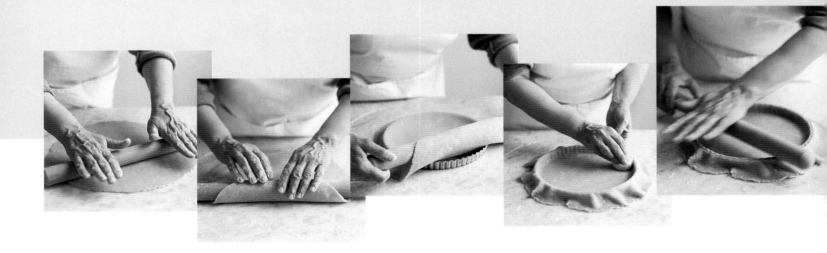

1 Preheat the oven to 200°C (400°F) Gas 6 – or 190°C (375°F) Gas 5 for pastries with a lot of sugar in them. Roll out the pastry as thinly as necessary to line the dish you are using.

Note Ovens vary so you may need slightly lower settings than these. Oven temperatures for Pâte Sucrée and Puff Pastry also vary (see page 26 and page 29).

2 To line a tart tin, roll the flour-dusted pastry around the rolling pin to help you pick it up – this will avoid stretching the pastry, which might shrink during cooking.

3 Lower the pastry over the tin and unroll to cover.

4 Use a small piece of extra pastry wrapped in a piece of clingfilm to help to push the pastry into the edges of the tin. Once this is done you can press the pastry up the sides of the tin.

5 Use the rolling pin to roll over the top – it will cut off any excess pastry very neatly. Alternatively, cut off the overhang with a very sharp knife.

I also like to press the pastry into the flutes of the ring after I've cut off the excess, to give a good shape.

6 Prick the base all over with a fork, then chill or freeze for 15 minutes to set the pastry.

7 Line with foil, baking parchment or all-purpose clingfilm (flicking the edges inwards towards the centre so that they don't catch on the pastry), then fill with baking beans.

Set on a baking sheet and bake blind in the centre of the oven for about 10–12 minutes.

8 Remove the foil, baking parchment or clingfilm and the baking beans and return the pastry case to the oven for a further 5–7 minutes to dry out completely.

9 To prevent pastry from becoming soggy from an particularly liquid filling, brush the blind-baked case with beaten egg – you can do this when it is hot or cold. Bake again for 5–10 minutes until set and shiny. This will also fill and seal any holes made when pricking before the blind baking.

10 If necessary, repeat the sealing process until an impervious layer has been built.

making small party tarts

Making your own little tarts takes less time than you think. They are very impressive, and are a good way of using up any leftover pastry if a large tart doesn't use a full quantity. Shortcrust pastries give a homemade feel, but for true finesse, use Pâte Brisée (page 24) for savoury tarts and Pâte Sucrée (page 26) for sweet ones. They can be frozen in the tin or cooked, cooled and stored in an airtight container.

1 Preheat the oven to 200°C (400°F) Gas 6 – or 190°C (375°F) Gas 5 if the pastry has a high sugar content. Roll out the pastry thinly on a floured work surface and use a plain or fluted pastry cutter to stamp out small rounds slightly larger than the holes in your tin.

2 Carefully ease each pastry round into the tin, avoiding stretching the pastry. Press into the base using a small piece of pastry wrapped in clingfilm. Prick the base with a fork, then chill or freeze for 15 minutes.

3 Line each base with all-purpose clingfilm or foil, then fill with baking beans. Bake blind for 5–10 minutes, depending on the size. Remove the clingfilm or foil and return to the oven for a further 1–2 minutes to dry out.

using filo pastry

Filo pastry is a paper-thin, almost see-through pastry from Greece. It is sold fresh or frozen in sheets rolled up in a packet. Look for the authentic Greek filo rather than supermarket own brands, which tend to be thicker and coarser.

The important thing to remember when using filo pastry is not to let it dry out. Once it dries out, it cracks and is impossible to use. Always keep it in a plastic bag or under a slightly damp tea towel or sheet of plastic film.

Cut all the pastry into the appropriate size at once and store in the plastic bag while you paint each sheet with melted butter to give it flavour and colour. Some people use olive oil, but I find butter is best.

Use as soon as the pastry is buttered, whether filling, rolling, folding or pressing into a tart mould.

Filo is baked at 200°C (400°F) Gas 6 to set it, then turned down to 190° (375°F) Gas 5 to finish and brown the pastry evenly. Don't cook it at a lower temperature or the pastry will become soggy.

lattice tops

The lattice top gives a pretty decorative finish to a tart, teasingly half-concealing what lies beneath. There are many ways of doing this by hand – you can simply arrange the strips over each other, interweave them, or twist them to give a barley-sugar effect. If this looks too fiddly and time-consuming, use a lattice cutter to create a lovely lacy effect. If there is no pastry rim, set a ring of pastry around the edge of the filled tart to keep the strips in place.

400 g pastry will line and lattice a 23 cm tart tin

Note You will need utensils such as a very sharp knife, a ruler or straight edge, or a lattice cutter (optional)

The classic method

1 Roll out the pastry thinly. Decide how many strips will fit across the tart. Cut into equal strips with the knife, using the ruler or edge as a guide.

2 If there is no rim or it is not wide enough to support the lattice, cut out a ring of dough to fit inside the edge of the tart. Dampen the edge, then start arranging the strips at equal intervals across the filled tart. If you are not sure about where to position the strips, lay them half-way across at first, folding them back so that they can be easily moved if necessary.

3 Set a second set of strips across the first, either interweaving them like basketwork, or simply setting them at right angles across the first set of strips.

4 Trim the edges of the strips for a neat finish.

decorative edges

There are countless ways of decorating pastry edges on a tart – many designs are steeped in tradition and specifically used for particular tarts. The simplest is the forked edge, followed by using the tip of a knife to create cuts and folds. The edge is normally brushed with milk or beaten egg to give a soft sheen or shiny glaze.

Using a lattice cutter

1 Roll out the dough to a size slightly larger than the tart. Roll the cutter the length of the dough, pressing firmly to make clean cuts.

2 Gently pull the lattice open and drape over a rolling pin. Lift carefully onto the tart, opening the mesh evenly. Press firmly around the edges to seal, trim off the excess and finish with a decorative edge (see right).

Fork edge

The edge of the pastry is marked by pressing the tines of the fork flat across the surface, so that the marks radiate outwards. Press quite hard to make deep indentations, then chill for 10 minutes to set.

Dog edge

These cuts look rather like a dog's floppy ears, hence the name! Using a sharp knife, make small cuts the width of the pastry edge about a thumb's breadth apart. Fold every alternate 'ear' over towards the centre of the tin and press the edge (not the fold) to seal. Chill for 10 minutes.

Devil edge

I call this design 'devil edge' because I think it looks jaggedly devilish! It is the traditional edge for a treacle tart. Using a sharp knife, make small cuts the width of the pastry edge about a thumb's breadth apart. Fold over every 'flap' diagonally onto itself towards the centre of the tin, pressing the tips (not the folds) downwards to seal. Chill for 10 minutes.

pâte brisée

This pastry is really the French version of an unsweetened shortcrust. It has a finer texture so should be rolled out much thinner – to about 3 mm. Sometimes unsweetened pâte brisée is used for fruit tarts that are baked for a long time, because other pastries with a high sugar content would scorch before the fruit was cooked. This pastry provides a firm, crisp support for the fruit. Don't be tempted to leave out the water in either this or the recipe for Pâte Sucrée (page 26) – it makes the pastry stronger and easier to handle in the end.

200 g plain flour

a large pinch of salt

100 g unsalted butter, diced, at room temperature

1 medium egg yolk

2½–3 tablespoons iced water

makes about 350 g pastry, enough to line a tart tin, 25 cm diameter or 6 tartlet tins, 9 cm diameter

The classic method

1 Sift the flour and salt into a mound on a clean work surface.

2 Make a well in the middle with your fist.

3 Put the butter and egg yolk into the well and using the fingers of one hand 'peck' the eggs and butter together until they resemble scrambled eggs.

4 Using a palette knife or pastry scraper, flick the flour over the egg mixture and chop through until almost amalgamated.

In the food processor

This method is useful if you are nervous about making pastry or have very hot hands. (I have increased the ingredients here so the quantity will work well in a food processor.)

250 g plain flour

1 teaspoon salt

125 g unsalted butter, softened

1 large egg yolk

2½–3 tablespoons iced water

5 Sprinkle with the water and chop again.

6 Bring together quickly with your hands. Knead lightly into a ball, then flatten slightly.

7 Wrap in clingfilm and chill for at least 30 minutes. Let it return to room temperature before rolling out.

1 Sift the flour and salt together onto a sheet of greaseproof paper.

2 Put the butter and egg yolk into a food processor and blend until smooth, then add the water and blend again.

3 Add the flour and salt and pulse until just mixed.

4 Transfer to a lightly floured work surface and knead gently until smooth. Form into a ball, flatten slightly and wrap in clingfilm.

5 Chill in the refrigerator for at least 30 minutes. Let the dough return to room temperature before rolling out.

pâte sucrée

This is the classic French sweet pastry sometimes known as pâte sablée or 'sandy pastry', because it has a fine crumbly texture when broken. Its high sugar content means that it can burn very easily – use a timer! It takes slightly longer to blind bake than other pastries – bake at the standard 190°C (375°) Gas 5 for 15 minutes, then reduce the temperature to 180°C (350°F) Gas 4 and cook for a further 10 minutes to dry out completely.

200 g plain flour

a pinch of salt

75 g caster or icing sugar

75 g unsalted butter, diced, at room temperature

2 medium egg yolks

½ teaspoon real vanilla essence

2–3 tablespoons iced water

makes about 400 g pastry, enough to line a tart tin, 25 cm diameter or 6 tartlet tins, 9 cm diameter

In the food processor

1 Sift the flour and salt onto a sheet of greaseproof paper.

2 Put the sugar, butter, egg yolks and vanilla essence into a food processor, then blend until smooth.

3 Add the water and blend again.

4 Add the flour to the food processor.

Pâte Sucrée can also be made by hand, as shown in the previous recipe Pâte Brisée on page 24.

5 Blend until just combined.

6 Transfer to a lightly floured work surface. Knead gently until the dough is smooth.

7 Form into a flattened ball, then wrap in clingfilm. Chill or freeze for at least 30 minutes.

Let return to room temperature before rolling out. This is quite a delicate pastry to roll, so be sure to use enough (but not too much) flour when rolling.

1 Sift flour, salt and sugar into a mound on a clean work surface.

2 Make a well in the middle with your fist.

3 Put the butter, egg yolks and vanilla essence into the well. Using the fingers of one hand, 'peck' the eggs and butter together until the mixture resembles creamy scrambled eggs.

4 Flick the flour over the egg mixture and chop it through with a palette knife or pastry scraper, until it is almost amalgamated but looking very lumpy.

5 Sprinkle with the water and chop again.

6 Bring together quickly with your hands. Knead lightly into a ball, then flatten slightly.

7 Wrap in clingfilm, then chill for at least 30 minutes before using. Let return to room temperature before rolling.

puff pastry

This is the most difficult of all the layered pastries but, once mastered, it is relatively easy to do as long as you stick to the rules of resting and chilling. It is worth the effort – the flavour and texture means it is like biting into a buttery cloud! Flaky pastry involves dotting a dough with lard and butter before rolling and folding. It is a more complicated version of rough puff, which I prefer. Unless otherwise stated, blind-bake puff pastries at 230°C (450°F) Gas 8, to enable it to rise quickly, then lower the oven to 200°C (400°F) Gas 6 for the final drying-out stage.

250 g plain or strong plain flour

¼ teaspoon salt

250 g butter, in 1 piece at cool room temperature*

1 teaspoon lemon juice

about 150 ml iced water

makes about 550 g pastry, enough to line a tart tin, 30 cm diameter

The butter must be malleable but not melting.

1 Sift the flour and salt into a large bowl.

2 Rub in one-quarter of the butter.

3 Sprinkle with the lemon juice and not quite all of the water.

4 Mix with the knife until the dough starts to come together in a lump. Add the rest of the water, 1 tablespoon at a time, if the mixture is dry.

(continued overleaf)

5 Tip this onto a floured work surface.

6 Knead lightly to form a smooth ball. Flatten the ball with the palm of your hand, then wrap the pastry in clingfilm and chill for about 30 minutes until firm.

7 Put the remaining butter between sheets of baking parchment, then roll or beat with a rolling pin to make a square about 1 cm thick.

8 Unwrap the pastry and roll out into a square large enough to wrap around the butter.

9 Put the butter in the centre of the pastry.

10 Bring the edges up and over to cover the butter completely.

11 Dust the rolling pin and both sides of the pastry parcel with flour.

Take the rolling pin and make 3 or 4 impressions on the surface of the dough parcel to start the pastry rolling.

12 Roll into a long rectangle three times longer than it is wide – you don't need exact measurements here but the pastry should be about 1 cm thick.

Remove any excess flour using a dry pastry brush.

13 Lightly mark the rectangle into 3 equal sections, using the blunt edge of a knife.

14 Fold the third that is closest to you up over the middle third.

(continued overleaf)

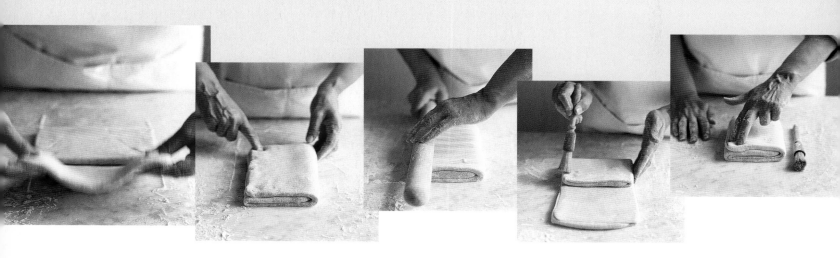

15 Bring the top third towards you over the folded two-thirds. (This is the first roll and fold.)

16 Give the pastry a quarter turn anti-clockwise so that it looks like a closed book, with the long open edge to the right. Make a finger mark in the pastry to remind you that you have rolled and folded it once (next time, make 2 marks and so on). Rewrap and chill for 15 minutes.

17 Return the pastry to the work surface in the closed-book position.

Seal the 3 edges lightly with a rolling pin to stop them sliding out of shape.

18 Now roll out, away from you in one direction only, until the pastry forms the same-sized rectangle as before. Fold in the same way as before, wiping off any excess flour with the pastry brush.

Note It is important to be consistent about the direction of rolling and folding in order to build up the leaves of the pastry; always start with the long open edge to your right.

19 Make two indentations in the the pastry (to indicate 2 roll-and-folds), then wrap and chill for 15 minutes. Do this rolling and folding 5 more times (a total of 7 rollings), then the pastry is ready to use.

Chill for 30 minutes before rolling to its final shape, then chill again for at least 30 minutes.

20 When the pastry has been cut to shape, the edges are 'knocked up' with the blade of a sharp knife to separate the layers and ensure a good rise.

rough puff pastry

This is a quick way to make good puff pastry. Needless to say, you must work very quickly, and it takes a little practice. Rolling and folding the pastry creates layers of pastry and pockets of butter. The cooked pastry will be buttery, puffy and light if made well: there is absolutely no comparison with bought puff pastry. Make a large quantity at one time and freeze the remainder – it is easier to make in bulk and you will always have some on hand when you need it. A dash of lemon juice is sometimes added with the water to strengthen the layers of dough.

250 g plain flour

a pinch of salt

150 g unsalted butter, chilled

about 150 ml iced water

makes about 550 g pastry, enough to line a tart tin, 30 cm diameter

1 Sift the flour and salt into a large bowl.

2 Quickly cut the butter into small cubes, about the size of the top of your little finger. Add to the flour mixture.

3 Stir the butter into the flour with a round-bladed knife so that it is evenly distributed.

4 Sprinkle the water over the surface, mixing in with knife as you do so.

(continued overleaf)

5 Mix with the knife until the dough starts to come together in a messy lump.

6 Tip onto a floured work surface. Knead lightly until it forms a streaky, rather lumpy ball. Flatten the ball with the palm of your hand, then wrap the pastry in clingfilm and chill for about 30 minutes until firm.

7 Unwrap and roll out away from you into a long rectangle that is three times longer than it is wide – no exact measurements needed here, but it should be about 1 cm thick.

Remove any excess flour with a dry pastry brush.

8 Lightly mark the pastry into 3 equal sections using a blunt knife.

9 Now fold the third closest to you up over the middle third.

10 Bring the top third towards you over the folded two-thirds.

11 Give the pastry a quarter turn anti-clockwise so that it looks like a closed book.

Seal the 3 edges lightly with a rolling pin to stop them sliding out of shape.

12 Now roll out, always away from you in one direction, until it is the same sized rectangle as before.

13 Fold in the same way as before.

14 Make a finger indentation on the pastry to indicate you that you have completed 1 roll and fold process, then wrap and chill for 15 minutes. Do this rolling and folding 4 more times (indenting it each time to indicate the number of roll and folds completed).

Chill for 30 minutes, then roll to its final shape. Chill again for at least 30 minutes.

cheat's rough puff pastry

A great friend showed me how to do this. It is really easy – but the butter must be very hard. It is made in exactly the same way as the rough puff pastry except that you freeze and grate the butter, then roll and fold the dough as quickly as you can. He swears that it is lighter made with margarine – I prefer using butter!

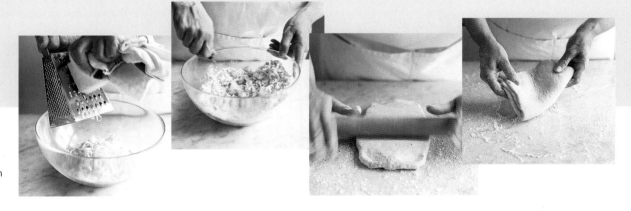

250 g plain flour

a pinch of salt

150 g unsalted butter, frozen

about 150 ml iced water

makes about 500 g pastry, enough to line a loose-based tart tin, 30 cm diameter

1 Sift the flour and salt into a large bowl.

2 Hold the butter in a tea towel and, using the large side of a box grater, quickly grate the butter into the flour.

3 Stir the butter into the flour with a round-bladed knife until evenly distributed.

4 Sprinkle the water over the surface, then mix with the knife until the dough starts to come together in a messy lump.

5 Tip this onto a floured work surface and knead lightly until it forms a streaky, rather lumpy ball.

6 Flatten the ball with the palm of your hand. Wrap in clingfilm and chill for 30 minutes until firm.

7 Unwrap and roll out away from you into a rectangle 3 times longer than it is wide – no exact measurements are needed here, but it should be about 1 cm thick.

8 Remove any excess flour with a pastry brush.

9 Lightly mark the pastry into 3 equal sections with a blunt knife.

10 Fold the third closest to you up over the middle third, then bring the top third towards you over the folded two-thirds.

11 Make a finger mark in the pastry to indicate you have completed 1 roll, then fold. Rewrap and chill for 15 minutes.

12 Repeat twice more (indenting each time with the number of roll and folds completed). Wrap and chill for 30 minutes.

13 Roll to the final shape, then chill for 30 minutes.

my just-push-it-in pastry
or pâte frolle (almond pastry)

This sweet almond pastry is made in both France and Italy. Overworked, it is tough – but properly made, it is crisp and light. It is almost impossible to roll out, so I shape it into a sausage, then wrap in clingfilm and chill until firm. I then slice it into thin rounds and push these into the base of the tin, pressing all over to make an even base.

200 g plain flour

a pinch of salt

75 g caster or icing sugar

75 g ground almonds

75 g unsalted butter, cubed, at room temperature

2 medium egg yolks

½ teaspoon real vanilla essence

2–3 tablespoons iced water

makes about 450 g pastry, enough to line a tart tin, 23–25 cm diameter

The classic way

1 Sift flour, salt and sugar into a mound on a clean work surface.

2 Sprinkle the almonds on top of the flour.

3 Make a well in the middle with your fist.

4 Put the butter, egg yolks and vanilla essence into the well. Using the fingers of one hand, 'peck' the eggs and butter together until the mixture resembles creamy scrambled eggs.

(continued overleaf)

5 Flick the flour over the egg mixture and chop it through with a palette knife, until it is almost amalgamated but still very lumpy.

6 Sprinkle with the water and chop again.

7 Bring together quickly with your hands and knead lightly, then shape into a thick sausage.

8 Wrap in clingfilm and chill for at least 2 hours.

9 Unwrap and cut into thin slices.

10 Push the slices into the base and sides of the tin, overlapping them very slightly and pushing together so that they form an even layer.

11 Chill or freeze for at least 30 minutes.

In the food processor

This method makes the whole process much easier – and no sticky mess on the table to clear up afterwards. It keeps the pastry cool, so is useful on a hot day, or if you have hot hands. As always, take care not to overwork the pastry as this can toughen it.

1 Sift the flour and salt onto a sheet of greaseproof paper, then add the almonds.

2 Put the sugar, butter, egg yolks and vanilla essence into a food processor and blend until smooth. Add the water and blend again.

3 Add the flour mixture and blend again until everything is just combined.

4 Transfer to a lightly floured work surface and knead gently until smooth. Form into a long sausage, then wrap in clingfilm. Chill in the refrigerator for at least 2 hours.

5 Cut into slices and push into the base and sides of the tin. Chill or freeze for 30 minutes.

savoury tarts

quiche lorraine

A classic tart from Alsace and Lorraine, and the forerunner of many copies. Made well and with the best ingredients, this simplest of dishes is food fit for the gods. I like to add a little grated Gruyère to the filling.

1 recipe Basic Shortcrust Pastry (page 13) or Cheat's Rough Puff Pastry chilled (page 39)

200 g bacon lardons or cubed pancetta

5 medium eggs

200 ml double cream or crème fraîche

freshly grated nutmeg, to taste

50 g Gruyère cheese, grated

sea salt and freshly ground black pepper

a tart tin, 23 cm diameter

foil or baking parchment and baking beans

serves 4–6

If using Basic Shortcrust Pastry, bring to room temperature. Preheat the oven to 200°C (400°F) Gas 6.

Roll out the pastry thinly on a lightly floured work surface and use to line the tart tin. Prick the base, chill or freeze for 15 minutes, then bake blind, following the method given on page 19.

Heat a non-stick frying pan and fry the bacon or pancetta until brown and crisp, then drain on kitchen paper. Scatter over the base of the pastry case.

Put the eggs and cream or crème fraîche into a bowl, beat well, and season with salt, pepper and nutmeg to taste. Carefully pour the mixture over the bacon and sprinkle with the Gruyère.

Bake for about 25 minutes until just set, golden brown and puffy. Serve warm or at room temperature.

onion, rosemary and roasted garlic tartlets

Toasting the whole garlic cloves in oil gives them a sweet nuttiness, and almost caramelizes them. They are blended into a custard with lots of rosemary, then cooked in the mini tartlet shells to make deliciously rustic appetizers. Serve with a big red wine to match the robust flavours.

½ recipe Rich Shortcrust Pastry (page 14) or Pâte Brisée (page 24)

onion and garlic filling

75 g butter

600 g sweet onions, sliced

1 teaspoon salt

300 ml double cream or crème fraîche

2 sprigs of rosemary

6 large garlic cloves

olive oil

4 medium egg yolks

freshly grated nutmeg, to taste

2 tablespoons chopped fresh rosemary

sea salt and freshly ground black pepper

30 Greek-style black olives, chopped, or rosemary sprigs, to finish

6 individual tartlet tins or 15 mini ones (you could use a mini muffin tin)

foil or baking parchment and baking beans

makes 6 tartlets or 12–15 mini tartlets

Bring the pastry to room temperature. Preheat the oven to 200°C (400°F) Gas 6. Roll out the pastry thinly on a lightly floured surface and use to line the tart tins, then prick the bases, chill or freeze for 15 minutes, and bake blind following the method on page 19.

Melt the butter in a large saucepan and add the onions, stirring to coat. Add a few tablespoons of water and the 1 teaspoon salt, and cover with a lid. Steam very gently for 30 minutes to 1 hour (trying not to look too often!) until meltingly soft. When the onions are cooked, remove the lid and cook for a few minutes to evaporate any excess liquid – the mixture should be quite thick. Let cool.

Put the cream or crème fraîche and rosemary leaves into a saucepan and heat until almost boiling. Remove from the heat and leave to infuse for as long as possible.

Put the garlic cloves into a small saucepan and just cover with olive oil. Simmer over gentle heat for 40 minutes or until the garlic is golden and soft.*

Remove the garlic from the oil (which you can keep to make salad dressings). Strain the cooled flavoured cream into a blender and add the cooked garlic and egg yolks. Season to taste with salt, pepper and nutmeg, and blend until smooth. Stir in the chopped rosemary.

Set the tartlet cases on a baking sheet. Spoon the cooled onions evenly into the cases, filling just half full. Pour the rosemary and garlic cream over the top. Bake for 15–20 minutes (depending on size) or until set and pale golden brown.

Serve warm, topped with chopped black olives or a sprig of rosemary.

***Note** To make a larger quantity of caramelized garlic cloves, wrap a whole unpeeled head of garlic in foil and roast at 190°C (375°F) Gas 5 for about 45 minutes until soft. Open the foil and squeeze the garlic out of the skins.

flamiche

(a melting leek tart from Belgium)

½ recipe Rich Shortcrust Pastry (page 14)
or Pâte Brisée (page 24)*

75 g butter

900 g leeks, split, well washed
and thickly sliced

1 teaspoon salt

4 medium egg yolks

300 ml double cream or crème fraîche

freshly grated nutmeg, to taste

sea salt and freshly ground black pepper

a tart tin, 20.5 cm diameter

a baking sheet

foil or baking parchment
and baking beans

serves 4–6

*Make the full amount and cook
2 cases, freezing 1 for later use.

There is nothing quite like the combination of meltingly soft sweet leeks, cream and pastry. This tart is perfect for a picnic served with some pâte and cold meats.

Bring the pastry to room temperature. Preheat the oven to 200°C (400°F) Gas 6.

Roll out the pastry thinly on a lightly floured work surface, then use to line the tart tin, prick the base, then chill or freeze for 15 minutes. Bake blind following the method on page 19.

Melt the butter in a large saucepan and add the leeks, stirring to coat. Add a few tablespoons of water and the 1 teaspoon salt, and cover with a lid. Steam very gently for at least 30 minutes (trying not to look too often!) until soft and melting. Remove the lid and cook for a few minutes to evaporate any excess liquid – the mixture should be quite thick. Let cool.

Put the egg yolks and cream or crème fraîche into a bowl, add salt, pepper and nutmeg to taste and beat well. Set the pastry case on a baking sheet. Spoon the cooled leeks evenly into the pastry case, fluffing them up a bit with a fork. Pour the eggs and cream mixture over the top.

Bake for 30 minutes or until set and pale golden brown. Serve warm.

roquefort tart

with walnut and toasted garlic dressing

Roquefort is a salty French blue cheese that's made with ewes' milk, but you could substitute any good-quality blue cheese. Walnuts are the perfect partner for blue cheese, especially when combined with the sweetly toasted slivers of garlic in this dressing.

1 recipe Pâte Brisée (page 24)

225 g cream or curd cheese (such as Philadelphia)

150 ml crème fraîche or double cream

3 medium eggs, beaten

175 g Roquefort or other good blue cheese

freshly ground black pepper

freshly grated nutmeg, to taste

3 tablespoons chopped fresh chives

walnut and toasted garlic dressing

3 garlic cloves

2 tablespoons olive oil

75 g walnut halves

1 tablespoon walnut oil

3 tablespoons chopped fresh parsley

a loose-based tart tin, 25 cm diameter

foil or baking parchment and baking beans

serves 6

Bring the pastry to room temperature. Preheat the oven to 200°C (400°F) Gas 6.

Roll out the pastry thinly on a lightly floured work surface, then use to line the tart tin. Prick the base, chill or freeze for 15 minutes, then bake blind following the method on page 19.

To make the filling, put the cream or curd cheese into a bowl and beat until softened. Beat in the crème fraîche or cream and the eggs. Crumble in the Roquefort and mix gently. Season with lots of black pepper and nutmeg. The cheese is salty, so you won't have to add extra salt. Stir in the chives and set aside.

Let the pastry case cool slightly and lower the oven to 190°C (375°F) Gas 5. Pour the filling into the case and bake for 30–35 minutes or until puffed and golden brown.

Meanwhile, to make the walnut and garlic dressing, slice the garlic into the thinnest of slivers. Heat the olive oil in a frying pan and add the garlic and walnuts. Stir-fry until the garlic is golden and the walnuts browned. Stir in the walnut oil and parsley.

Serve the tart warm or at room temperature with the warm walnut and garlic dressing.

goats' cheese, leek and walnut tart

This light, creamy open tart is easy to make because there is no need to line a tin or bake blind – simply roll out the pastry and top like a pizza. Goats' cheese and walnuts are a great combination, especially combined with soft earthy leeks.

½ recipe Puff Pastry (page 29)*
or 250 g frozen puff pastry, thawed

50 g butter

4 small leeks, trimmed and sliced

200 g goats' cheese log with rind, sliced

sea salt and freshly ground black pepper

extra chopped fresh parsley, to serve

walnut paste

125 g walnut pieces

3 garlic cloves, crushed

6 tablespoons walnut oil

3 tablespoons chopped fresh parsley

a 28 cm dinner plate

a baking sheet

serves 4–6

*If using homemade Puff Pastry, make the full recipe and freeze the remainder for later use.

Preheat the oven to 200°C (400°F) Gas 6. Roll out the pastry thinly on a lightly floured work surface and cut out a 28 cm circle using the dinner plate as a template. Set on a baking sheet and chill or freeze for at least 15 minutes.

Melt the butter in a large saucepan and add the leeks, stirring to coat. Add a few tablespoons of water and a teaspoon of salt, and cover with a lid. Steam very gently for at least 20 minutes (trying not to look too often!) until almost soft. Remove the lid and cook for a few minutes to evaporate any excess liquid. Let cool.

For the walnut paste, blend the walnuts and garlic in a food processor with 2 tablespoons water. Beat in the walnut oil and stir in the parsley. Spread this over the pastry, avoiding the rim.

Spoon the leeks into the pastry base and top with the slices of goats' cheese. Sprinkle with any remaining walnut paste. Season with salt and freshly ground black pepper and sprinkle with olive oil. Bake for 20 minutes until the pastry is golden and the cheese bubbling and brown.

Sprinkle with more parsley and serve immediately.

1 recipe Rich Shortcrust Pastry (page 14) or Pâte Brisée (page 24)

slow-roasted tomatoes

12–15 large ripe cherry tomatoes

2 finely chopped garlic cloves

1 tablespoon dried oregano

4 tablespoons olive oil

sea salt and freshly ground black pepper

herby cheese filling

80 g full-fat soft cheese with garlic and herbs (such as Boursin)

1 large egg, beaten

150 ml double cream

4 tablespoons chopped fresh mixed herbs (such as parsley, basil, marjoram or chives)

75 g feta cheese

tiny sprigs of thyme or cut chives, to finish

sea salt and freshly ground black pepper

a plain biscuit cutter, 6 cm diameter

2 mini muffin tins, 12 holes each

foil or baking parchment and baking beans

makes 24 tartlets

Tiny tartlets are great to serve at a drinks party. They look stunning and have a secret pocket of feta cheese lurking in the creamy, herby filling underneath the tomatoes. Make double quantity of the roasted tomatoes – they keep well in the refrigerator and are great in salads.

slow-roasted tomato and herb tartlets with feta

Bring the pastry to room temperature. Preheat the oven to 200°C (400°F) Gas 6.

Roll out the pastry as thinly as possible on a lightly floured work surface. Use the biscuit cutter to stamp out 24 circles. Line the muffin tin holes with the pastry circles, then prick the bases and chill or freeze for 15 minutes. Bake blind following the method on page 19, then remove from the tins and let cool.*

Turn the oven down to 160°C (325°F) Gas 3. Cut the tomatoes in half around the middle. Arrange cut side up on a baking sheet. Put the chopped garlic, oregano, olive oil and lots of ground pepper into a bowl and mix well, then spoon or brush over the cut tomatoes. Bake slowly in the oven for about 1½–2 hours, checking every now and then. They should be slightly shrunk and still a brilliant red colour – if too dark, they will taste bitter.**

Put the soft cheese into a bowl, add the egg, cream and chopped herbs and beat until smooth. Season well. Cut the feta into 24 small cubes that will fit inside the pastry cases.

When ready to bake, set the cases on a baking sheet, put a cube of feta in each one and top up with the garlic and herb mixture. Bake in the preheated oven at 180°C (350°F) Gas 4 for about 15–20 minutes or until the filling is set. Top each with a tomato half, a sprinkle of the cooking juices and a thyme sprig or chive stem. Serve warm.

*Note The pastry cases will keep for up to 1 week in an airtight tin, but reheat to crisp them up before filling.

**Note Use the tomatoes straight away or pack in a storage jar and cover with olive oil.

potato and parmesan tart with chives

Real comfort food for a miserable wet weekend! This is a deliciously creamy tart, which makes an unusual supper dish served with smoked salmon or a crunchy Caesar salad.

1 recipe Rich Shortcrust Pastry (page 14)

900 g waxy potatoes, such as Desirée, thinly sliced*

50 g butter, cut into pieces

125 g freshly grated Parmesan

4 tablespoons chopped chives

freshly grated nutmeg, to taste

1 medium egg, beaten

300 ml double cream

sea salt and freshly ground black pepper

a deep springform tart tin, 20.5 cm diameter or any suitable dish with a 1 litre capacity

foil or baking parchment and baking beans

serves 4–6

Do not rinse the potatoes – their starch will help to thicken the cream.

Bring the pastry to room temperature. Preheat the oven to 200°C (400°F) Gas 6.

Roll out the pastry thinly on a lightly floured work surface. Use the pastry to line the tin or dish (this can be a little tricky, so be patient and take your time), then prick the base. Chill or freeze for 15 minutes, then bake blind following the method on page 19.

After baking blind, turn down the oven to 160°C (325°F) Gas 3. Reserve 50 g of the Parmesan. Layer the sliced potatoes and butter in the baked case, seasoning each layer with some of the remaining Parmesan, chives, nutmeg, salt and pepper.

Put the egg and cream into a bowl, beat well, then pour over the potatoes. Sprinkle the reserved 50 g Parmesan over the top. Bake for about 1 hour (it may take up to 15 minutes longer, depending on the type of potato used) or until the potatoes are tender and the top is dark golden brown.

Let cool for 10 minutes, then remove from the springform tin or dish. Alternatively, serve straight from the dish!

Note You could speed up the cooking time by precooking the filling in the microwave, but it will not look quite as good. Mix the sliced potatoes, pieces of butter, 75 g of the Parmesan, nutmeg, half the cream, salt and pepper in a non-metallic bowl. Cover, leaving a small hole for steam to escape, and microwave for 10 minutes on HIGH. Mix in the remaining cream and egg. Carefully spoon the mixture into the pastry case, sprinkling with chives as you go. Finish with the remaining Parmesan cheese and bake for about 30 minutes until tender.

A wickedly creamy tart that puffs up during baking, and is filled with the spring flavours of fresh asparagus and waxy new potatoes encased in a crisp nutmeg and dill pastry shell.

chunky new potato and asparagus tart

1 recipe Dill and Nutmeg Pastry (page 15)

500 g small new potatoes (or other waxy potatoes)

400 g fresh asparagus

4 whole eggs plus 2 yolks, beaten

150 ml crème fraîche

sea salt and freshly ground black pepper

a little olive oil, to serve

a rectangular tart tin , 20 x 28 cm

a baking sheet

foil or baking parchment and baking beans

serves 6–8

Bring the pastry to room temperature. Preheat the oven to 200°C (400°F) Gas 6.

Roll out the pastry thinly on a lightly floured work surface, then use to line the tart tin. Prick the base, chill or freeze for 15 minutes, then bake blind following the method given on page 19.

Lower the oven to 190°C (375°F) Gas 5. Meanwhile, boil the potatoes in salted water for 20 minutes until tender. While boiling, trim the asparagus and cut into 4 cm lengths. Reserve the tips. Add the asparagus stems to the potatoes 6 minutes before the potatoes are cooked.

Drain and refresh the vegetables in cold water, then thickly slice the potatoes. Put the eggs and crème fraîche into a bowl, whisk well, then season with salt and pepper.

Arrange the potatoes and asparagus over the base of the pastry case and pour in the egg mixture. Set on a baking sheet and bake in the preheated oven for 25–30 minutes until puffed up and golden brown.

Meanwhile, cook the reserved asparagus tips in boiling salted water until tender, then drain and refresh. Toss the tips in a little olive oil and serve a spoonful with each portion. Serve warm.

creamy aubergine tart with slow-roasted cherry tomatoes

paprika and gruyère pastry

75 g butter

175 g plain flour

½ teaspoon sweet paprika

½ teaspoon dry mustard powder

55 g freshly grated Gruyère cheese

1 medium egg yolk

2 tablespoons iced water

sea salt and freshly ground black pepper

slow-roasted tomatoes

500 g large ripe cherry tomatoes

2 garlic cloves, finely chopped

1 tablespoon dried oregano

4 tablespoons olive oil

sea salt and freshly ground black pepper

aubergine filling

2 medium aubergines

2 garlic cloves, crushed

½ teaspoon smoked sweet paprika

1 tablespoon dried oregano

3 medium eggs, beaten

sea salt and freshly ground black pepper

2–3 tablespoons olive oil, to finish

a baking sheet

*a loose-based rectangular tart tin,
25 x 15 cm*

*foil or baking parchment
and baking beans*

serves 6

The combination of creamy aubergine, garlic and tomatoes sings of the sun. This is the perfect tart to eat on a hot summer's day, accompanied by a bitter leafy salad and a lot of warm chatter.

To prepare the slow-roasted tomatoes, preheat the oven to 160°C (325°F) Gas 3. Cut the tomatoes in half around the middle and arrange them cut side up on a baking sheet.

Put the garlic, oregano, olive oil, salt and pepper into a bowl and mix well. Spoon or brush over the cut tomatoes. Bake slowly in the oven for about 2 hours, checking every now and then. They should be slightly shrunk and still a brilliant red colour – if too dark, they will taste bitter. (You can use the tomatoes straight away or pack into a jar and cover with olive oil.)

To make the pastry, rub the butter into the flour until it resembles fine breadcrumbs. Stir in the paprika, mustard, Gruyère, salt and pepper. Mix the egg with 2 tablespoons cold water and mix into the flour for a soft dough. (Sprinkle with a little more water if the mixture is too dry.)

Knead until smooth, wrap in clingfilm and chill for 30 minutes. Use to line the tart tin, then prick the base and chill or freeze for 15 minutes. Preheat the oven to 200°C (400°F) Gas 6 and bake blind following the method given on page 19.

To make the filling, prick the aubergines all over and bake in the oven for 45 minutes, or until soft. Remove from the oven and let cool. (Or prick each aubergine in 2–3 places and microwave on HIGH for 12 minutes until soft.)

Turn down the oven to 180°C (350°F) Gas 4. Halve the aubergines and scoop out the flesh into a food processor. Add the garlic, paprika, oregano, eggs and salt and pepper to taste, then blend until smooth. Pour into the pastry case and bake for about 25 minutes or until set.

Remove from the oven and let cool. Arrange the roasted tomatoes over the surface to cover completely. Sprinkle with the olive oil (or use oil from the jar if you have stored the tomatoes), then serve.

These are completely vegetarian, and completely delicious! To get a really smoky barbecue flavour into the aubergines, try grilling or barbecuing them whole. You will have to turn them often to cook them evenly – make sure they are very charred and completely soft before using.

aubergine, mushroom and coriander tartlets

1 recipe Basic Shortcrust Pastry (page 13) or 350 g bought fresh or frozen ready-rolled shortcrust pastry

aubergine, mushroom and coriander filling

2 medium aubergines

3 tablespoons olive oil

2 shallots, finely chopped

2 tablespoons crushed coriander seeds

225 g large flat mushrooms, finely chopped

3–4 tablespoons white wine

1 medium egg, beaten

75 ml double cream

60 g chopped fresh coriander

sea salt and freshly ground black pepper

aubergine garnish

1 small aubergine

vegetable oil, for frying

8 tartlet tins, 9 cm diameter

a baking sheet

foil or baking parchment and baking beans

a deep-fryer

makes 8 tartlets

Bring the pastry to room temperature. Preheat the oven to 200°C (400°F) Gas 6. Roll the pastry as thinly as you dare on a lightly floured work surface, then use to line the tartlet tins. Prick the bases, chill or freeze for 15 minutes, then bake blind following the method given on page 19.

Put the whole aubergines onto a baking sheet and bake for about 45 minutes or until soft and beginning to char.*

Heat the oil in a medium saucepan and add the shallots and coriander seeds. Cook gently for 5 minutes until soft and golden. Stir in the mushrooms and wine and cook over high heat for 10 minutes or until all the liquid has evaporated.

Remove the aubergines from the oven. Split them open and scoop out the flesh. Chop the flesh coarsely and beat into the mushroom mixture. Beat in the egg and cream. Stir in the chopped coriander and season well with salt and pepper. Spoon the mixture into the tartlet shells, then bake in a preheated oven at 190°C (375°F) Gas 5 for 15–20 minutes, or until lightly set. Remove from the oven and serve warm or at room temperature.

To make the aubergine garnish, cut the small aubergine into paper-thin slices using a mandoline or very sharp knife. Cut into smaller strips if necessary. Heat the oil to 180°C (350°F) in a wok or deep-fryer, add the aubergine and fry until lightly browned. Drain on kitchen paper, then use to top the tartlets before serving.

***Note** Alternatively, you can cook a whole aubergine in the microwave by piercing it few times, wrapping in kitchen paper and cooking on HIGH for 10–12 minutes. It won't have that smoky flavour, but will be very pale and creamy inside.

dark mushroom and tarragon tart

1 recipe Cheese Shortcrust Pastry (page 15)

75 g unsalted butter

1 onion, sliced

450 g dark open mushrooms, sliced

freshly squeezed juice of 1 lemon

2 tablespoons chopped fresh tarragon

200 g mascarpone cheese, softened

3 large eggs, beaten

sea salt and freshly ground black pepper

garlic crunch topping

55 g butter

150 g stale breadcrumbs

3 garlic cloves, chopped

finely grated zest of 1 unwaxed lemon

3 tablespoons chopped fresh parsley

a deep, fluted tart tin, 25 cm diameter

foil or baking parchment and baking beans

serves 6–8

Large dark mushrooms are full of flavour – the darker, the better. This tart has a creamy filling laced with tarragon and lemon. The garlicky crunchy topping turns it into a giant version of a stuffed mushroom – but more sophisticated! Serve with a fresh tomato salad.

Bring the pastry to room temperature. Preheat the oven to 200°C (400°F) Gas 6.

Roll out the pastry thinly on a lightly floured work surface. Use to line the tart tin, then chill or freeze for 15 minutes and bake blind following the method given on page 19.

Melt the butter in a frying pan, add the onion and fry until soft and golden. Add the mushrooms, lemon juice, salt and pepper, then fry over a medium heat for 5 minutes until the mushrooms are tender and the liquid has evaporated. Stir in the tarragon, then let the mixture cool slightly.

To make the topping, melt the butter in a frying pan, add the breadcrumbs, garlic, lemon zest and parsley and fry over brisk heat until the breadcrumbs begin to crisp but not colour too much. Tip the mixture into a bowl.

Put the mascarpone and eggs into a bowl and beat well. Stir in the mushroom mixture. Pour into the pastry case, then sprinkle with the topping and bake for 20–25 minutes until set, crisp and golden on top. Serve warm.

pissaladière

(Provençal tomato and onion pizza)

yeast pastry

10 g fresh yeast*

a pinch of sugar

200 g plain flour

55 g chilled butter, cubed

1 medium egg, beaten

a pinch of salt

olive oil, for greasing

herby onion filling

3 tablespoons olive oil

1.5 kg mild onions, thinly sliced

3 garlic cloves, chopped

2 teaspoons dried Herbes de Provence

tomato sauce

800 g canned chopped tomatoes

3 tablespoons tomato purée

2 tablespoons olive oil

1 teaspoon harissa (chilli-spice paste)

150 ml white wine

sea salt and freshly ground black pepper

to finish

15 anchovy fillets in oil,
halved lengthways

olive oil, for sprinkling

18 very good black olives

a Swiss roll tin, 33 x 20 cm

serves 6

*To use easy-blend dried yeast, mix
1 teaspoon with the flour, rub in the
butter, then continue as the main recipe.*

This Provençal version of Italian pizza is seen in every *boulangerie* in the Midi. There are many variations, and I've distilled them here into one perfect picnic food. You can use any good olives but I like the oven-dried Greek-style ones.

To make the onion filling, heat the oil in a large saucepan, add the onions and garlic and 3 tablespoons of water. Cover and cook over gentle heat for about 1 hour or until meltingly soft, but not coloured.** Stir the onions occasionally and watch they do not burn. Stir in the herbs, then set a sieve over a bowl and tip the onions into the sieve. Reserve the caught juices for the yeast pastry.

To make the pastry, cream the fresh yeast and sugar in a bowl, then whisk in 3 tablespoons of the reserved onion liquid. Leave for 10 minutes until frothy.

Sift the flour into a bowl and rub in the butter. Make a well in the centre and add the egg, yeast mixture and salt. Mix until it starts to come together, then transfer to a floured work surface and knead until smooth. Oil the bowl. Return the dough to the oiled bowl and put the bowl inside a polythene bag. Let rise for about 1 hour or until doubled in size.

To make the tomato sauce, put all the ingredients into a saucepan, mix well and bring to the boil. Simmer uncovered for about 1 hour, stirring occasionally until well reduced and very thick. Season well and set aside.

Preheat the oven to 190°C (375°F) Gas 5. Punch down the dough, knead, then roll out onto a lightly floured surface. Use to line the Swiss roll tin, bringing the dough well up the edges.

Spread the tomato sauce over the base and cover with the onions. Arrange the anchovy fillets in a lattice over the onions. Sprinkle with olive oil and bake for 1 hour until the pastry is golden and crisp.

Dot with the olives and serve warm or at room temperature.

Note You can cook the onions quickly in a microwave. Toss in the olive oil and put into a non-metallic bowl. Cover, leaving a small gap for the steam to escape, then microwave on HIGH for 10 minutes. Continue as for the conventional method.

spicy crab in filo cups

9 sheets filo pastry, about A4 paper size

50 g butter, melted

spicy crab filling

200 g canned white crab meat in brine, drained

75 g canned water chestnuts, drained and finely chopped or sliced

3 cm fresh ginger, peeled and cut into fine strips

2 spring onions, trimmed and finely sliced

finely grated zest and juice of 1 unwaxed lime

1 garlic clove, crushed

½ fresh red chilli, deseeded and finely chopped

2 teaspoons sesame oil

2 tablespoons chopped fresh coriander

sea salt and freshly ground black pepper

3 mini muffin tins, 12 holes each, brushed with melted butter

makes about 36

These delicate bites are as light as air, but packed with fresh Asian flavours. I tend to use canned white crab meat from the Pacific for these – not only does it taste very good, but there is no shell or messy bits to deal with if catering for a large number of people. It is also much cheaper than fresh.

Preheat the oven to 180°C (350°F) Gas 4.

Unroll the filo and cut the stack into 108 squares, each measuring 7 x 7 cm. To do this, keep the sheets stacked on top of each other, then mark the top sheet into 12 squares. Cut down through all the layers, giving 108 squares. Pile into 2–3 stacks and keep beside you in a plastic bag.

To make a filo cup, take 3 squares of filo, brush each with melted butter and lay one on top of the other, so that the points make a star, and do not touch each other. Quickly but gently press into one of the holes of the prepared muffin tin, so the points of the filo shoot upwards like a handkerchief. Repeat with all the remaining filo until you have 36 cups.

Bake in the oven for about 8–10 minutes until golden. Remove, let cool in the tin, then carefully remove to a tray (they are very fragile).

Put the crab into a bowl and fluff up with a fork. Stir in the water chestnuts, ginger and spring onions. In a separate bowl, mix the lime zest and juice, crushed garlic, chilli and sesame oil, and season to taste. Mix this into the crab mixture (this can be done up to 4 hours in advance), then stir in the coriander.

Fill the cups with the crab mixture just before serving (they can go a little soggy if they are kept too long).

crab and sweet pickled chilli tart

The sweet and salty taste of fresh crab (if you can get it) mixed with mild red chillies pickled in sweet vinegar is fantastic. They seem made for each other. Serve this with an avocado salsa or just plain sliced avocado dressed with a coriander vinaigrette.

1 recipe Cheese Shortcrust Pastry (page 15)

chilli crab filling

2 tablespoons olive oil

a bunch of spring onions, sliced

6 medium eggs

300 ml double cream

1 tablespoon Dijon mustard

500 g fresh or frozen white crabmeat, thawed and drained

8 mild, sweet pickled red chilli peppers, deseeded and roughly chopped

100 g freshly grated Parmesan

freshly ground black pepper

a loose-based tart tin, 25 diameter, 3 cm deep

a baking sheet

foil or baking parchment and baking beans

serves 6–8

Bring the pastry to room temperature. Preheat the oven to 200°C (400°F) Gas 6.

On a lightly floured work surface, roll the pastry out to a thickness of 3 mm and use to line the tart tin. Chill or freeze for 15 minutes, then bake blind following the method given on page 19. Let cool.

Reduce the oven temperature to 180°C (350°F) Gas 4. Heat the olive oil in a pan and fry the spring onions until softened, but not coloured. Let cool slightly.

Put the eggs, cream and mustard into a bowl and whisk well. Stir in the crab, cooked spring onions, sweet chilli peppers and Parmesan, then season with plenty of black pepper. Spoon into the pastry shell and level the surface.

Set on a baking sheet and bake for about 45 minutes until just firm. Serve warm or at room temperature.

salmon, dill and parmesan tart with pickled cucumber

1 recipe Rich Shortcrust Pastry (page 14) or Pâte Brisée (page 24)

salmon and dill filling

450 g fresh salmon fillets (with or without skin)

300 ml double cream

75 g smoked salmon pieces (scraps will do, but cut off any brown bits)

3 medium eggs, beaten

3 tablespoons chopped fresh dill

25 g freshly grated Parmesan cheese

sea salt and freshly ground black pepper

cucumber topping

2 large cucumbers

1 tablespoon sea salt

1 tablespoon caster sugar

100 ml white wine or cider vinegar

2 tablespoons chopped fresh dill

freshly ground white pepper

extra dill sprigs, to garnish

a tart tin, 25 cm diameter

a baking sheet

foil or baking parchment and baking beans

serves 6–8

I make this tart extra special by blending in a little smoked salmon (you could also use gravadlax) at the same time as the eggs and cream. This gives the tart a mysterious, slightly smoky flavour and a velvety texture.

Bring the pastry to room temperature. Preheat the oven to 200°C (400°F) Gas 6.

Roll out the pastry thinly on a lightly floured work surface, then use to line the tart tin. Chill or freeze for 15 minutes, then bake blind following the method given on page 19. Remove from the oven and reduce the oven temperature to 190°C (375°F) Gas 5.

Put the salmon fillets into a shallow pan and cover with cold water. Add a little salt and bring slowly to the boil. Just before the water boils, turn off the heat and leave the salmon in the water until it is cold – by then it will be cooked and very moist. Lift it out of the water and drain well. Peel off any skin and check for any bones. Flake coarsely.

Put the cream into a blender, add the smoked salmon and eggs, then blend until smooth. Season well with salt and pepper and stir in the dill. Sprinkle the salmon flakes over the base of the tart and pour in the smoked salmon and cream mixture. Sprinkle with the Parmesan, set on a baking sheet and bake in the preheated oven for 25 minutes, until just set. Remove from the oven and let cool completely.

Meanwhile, to make the cucumber topping, peel the cucumber, then slice as thinly as possible using a mandoline or a food processor. Spread in a colander and sprinkle with the salt, mixing well. Stand the colander on a plate and leave to drain for 30 minutes. Rinse well and squeeze the excess moisture out of the cucumber. Spread the cucumber over a large plate.

Dissolve the sugar in the vinegar and stir in the dill. Pour this over the cucumber and let marinate for at least 1 hour before serving.

To serve, drain the cucumber well and arrange it casually over the top of the salmon tart. Grind over lots of white pepper, top with dill sprigs, then serve immediately. Any extra salad can be served on the side.

smoked salmon, vodka and soured cream aspic tartlets

250 g Rich Shortcrust Pastry (page 14)
or Pâte Brisée (page 24) •

flavoured aspic

1 sheet of leaf gelatine

150 ml light fish stock

1–2 tablespoons lemon-flavoured vodka

2 tablespoons chopped fresh chives

smoked salmon filling

60 ml sour cream

90 g smoked salmon, chopped
(or avruga or keta caviar)

whole chives, to garnish

a plain biscuit cutter, 6 cm diameter

2 mini muffin tins, 12 holes each

*foil or baking parchment
and baking beans*

makes 24 tartlets

**Make up the full amount and freeze the
rest for later use.*

Make these pretty little tartlets for a special occasion – they simply explode with fabulous flavours. I usually make these with smoked salmon, but use avruga (herring roe prepared like caviar) if you can find it – its almost smoky taste is just perfect with the hidden sour cream and chives.

Bring the pastry to room temperature. Preheat the oven to 200°C (400°F) Gas 6.

Roll out the pastry as thinly as possible on a lightly floured work surface, then stamp out 24 circles with the biscuit cutter. Use these to line the holes of the mini muffin tins. Prick the bases and chill or freeze for 15 minutes. Bake blind using the method given on page 19, remove from the tins and cool.**

To make the flavoured aspic, soak the leaf gelatine in cold water for 2–3 minutes until soft. Warm the fish stock, then stir in the drained gelatine until dissolved. Add the vodka. Let cool until syrupy but still pourable, then stir in the chives.

Arrange the pastry cases on a tray and add ½ teaspoon sour cream to each tartlet. Cover with a mound of smoked salmon (or a little avruga or keta caviar), then spoon in enough aspic to fill to the top of the pastry. Put in the refrigerator for 15–20 minutes to set, then garnish each one with a couple of thin chive stems. Serve immediately.

****Note** You can keep the cases in an airtight tin for up to 1 week, but reheat to crisp them up before filling.

There is a fabulous blend of flavours in the filling. The mascarpone is dotted onto the sausage mixture before the onions are piled on top – so it just melts in.

sausage, sun-dried tomato and potato tart

with golden onions

1 recipe Pâte Brisée (page 24)

sausage and onion filling

3 tablespoons olive oil

3 onions, thinly sliced

2 garlic cloves, finely chopped

200 g potatoes, chopped

350 g best (preferably Toulouse) fresh pork sausages, skinned

1 tablespoon plain flour

2–3 tablespoons tomato purée

12 sun-dried tomato halves in oil, chopped

1 teaspoon dried chilli flakes

2 teaspoons dried Herbes de Provence

150 g mascarpone cheese

sea salt and freshly ground black pepper

a tart tin, 24 cm diameter, 4 cm deep

foil or baking parchment and baking beans

serves 4–6

Bring the pastry to room temperature. Preheat the oven to 200°C (400°F) Gas 6.

Roll out the pastry on a lightly floured work surface, then use to line the tart tin. Prick the base, then chill or freeze for 15 minutes. Bake blind following the method given on page 19.

To make the filling, heat the oil in a large saucepan, add the onions, garlic and 3 tablespoons water. Cover and cook over gentle heat for about 1 hour or until meltingly soft but not coloured. Stir the onions occasionally and watch for catching.* Let cool.

Blanch the potatoes in boiling salted water for 1 minute, then drain and set aside. Heat a non-stick frying pan and add the sausage meat, breaking it up with a fork or wooden spoon as it cooks and browns.

After about 5 minutes, stir in the flour, tomato purée, sun-dried tomatoes, chilli, herbs, and salt and pepper to taste. Cook for another 5 minutes, then stir in the potatoes. Spoon this into the pastry case and dot small spoonfuls of the mascarpone over the surface. Cover with a layer of the cooked onions, then bake for 25 minutes until the onions are golden.

***Note** You can cook the onions quickly in a microwave. Toss in the olive oil and set in a non-metallic bowl. Cover, leaving a small gap for the steam to escape, then microwave on HIGH for 10 minutes. Continue as for the conventional method.

sweet tarts

This is a tart filled with an uncooked lemon curd and baked in the oven until just firm. This recipe comes from my sister Jacks, who has a reputation for her fantastic lemon tarts. She has made really tiny ones for champagne receptions and weddings – if you are making bite-sized morsels, the pastry must be wonderfully thin so that they melt in the mouth.

classic lemon tart

1 recipe Sweet Rich Shortcrust Pastry (page 14, see note)

1 egg, beaten, to seal the pastry

crème fraîche, to serve (optional)

lemon filling

6 large eggs

350 g caster sugar

finely grated zest and strained juice of 4 juicy unwaxed lemons

125 g unsalted butter, melted

a loose-based fluted tart tin, 23 cm diameter

a baking sheet

serves 8

Bring the pastry to room temperature. Preheat the oven to 190°C (375°F) Gas 5.

Roll out the pastry thinly on a lightly floured work surface, and use to line the tart tin. Chill or freeze for 15 minutes, then bake blind following the method given on page 19. Brush with beaten egg, then bake again for 5–10 minutes until set and shiny to prevent the filling from making the pastry soggy.

Lower the oven to 150°C (300°F) Gas 2. To make the lemon filling, put the eggs, sugar, lemon zest and juice, and butter into a food processor and blend until smooth.

Set the baked tart shell on a baking sheet and pour in the filling. Bake in the oven for about 1 hour (it may need a little longer, depending on your oven) until just set. Remove from the oven and let cool completely before serving.

Serve at room temperature, maybe with a spoonful of crème fraîche.

Note For a special occasion you can decorate this tart with candied shreds of lemon zest. Peel the zest only from 3 or 4 lemons, leaving behind any white pith. Cut the zest into very fine shreds with a very sharp knife. Make a sugar syrup by boiling 75 g caster sugar with 150 ml water. Stir in the shreds and simmer for about 10 minutes until tender and almost transparent. Carefully lift out of the syrup, drain and sprinkle around the edge of the tart while still warm, to form a ring. Cool before serving.

I have been making this tart since I started cooking, at the tender age of eight – it used to be my *pièce de résistance*! Blending the sugar with large peelings of lemon zest transfers all the essential oils to the sugar and gives a wonderful aroma to the tart. Using cottage cheese instead of cream cheese gives a lighter texture and will cut the calories.

simple lemon cheese tart

1 recipe Sweet Rich Shortcrust Pastry (page 14, see note)

1 unwaxed lemon

75 g caster sugar

350 g cream cheese or full-fat soft cheese such as Philadelphia

1 medium egg, plus 3 egg yolks

2 teaspoons real vanilla essence

a loose-based tart tin, 23 cm diameter

serves 4–6

Bring the pastry to room temperature. Preheat the oven to 190°C (375°F) Gas 5.

Roll out the pastry on a lightly floured work surface and use to line the tart tin. Prick the base, then chill or freeze for 15 minutes. Bake blind following the method given on page 19. Let cool.

Peel the zest from the lemon leaving behind any white pith, and squeeze the juice. Put the zest and sugar into a food processor or small blender, and blend until the sugar and zest mixture looks damp.

Add the lemon juice and blend again – the lemon zest should be completely dissolved into the sugar. Add the cheese, egg yolks, whole egg and vanilla essence. Blend until smooth and pour into the baked case.

Bake for about 25 minutes until just set and lightly browned on top. Remove from the oven and let cool. Serve at room temperature.

This unusual chocolate and almond biscuit crust is the perfect foil for a sharp lemon and almond filling.

lemon and almond tart with chocolate amaretti crust

250 g amaretti biscuits or Italian ratafias

50 g dark chocolate, grated or chopped

75 g butter, melted

lemon almond filling

3 unwaxed lemons

4 large eggs

120 g sugar

120 g unsalted butter, melted

120 g ground almonds

150 g crème fraîche

*a deep tart tin,
23 cm diameter, 3 cm deep*

a baking sheet

serves 6–8

Preheat the oven to 180°C (350°F) Gas 4.

Put the amaretti biscuits or ratafias into a food processor and blend until finely crushed. Add the chocolate and blend again. Pour in the melted butter and blend until well mixed and coming together.

Put the tart tin onto a baking sheet. Press the mixture evenly over the base and sides of the tart tin (a potato masher and the back of a small spoon will help here). Bake for 10 minutes to set the base. Remove from the oven and press the puffed-up crust down again.

Finely grate the zest from the lemons and squeeze and strain the juice. Beat the eggs in a bowl and whisk in the lemon zest and juice, sugar, melted butter and ground almonds. Pour into the amaretti case and bake for 25 minutes until set and very lightly brown on top.

Cool, then spread with the crème fraîche and serve at room temperature.

In these delicious little tarts, a zesty lemon meringue puffs up like a cloud over a sea of blueberries, then sets to a featherlight cooked mousse. Irresistible!

blueberry and lemon cloud tartlets

1 recipe Pâte Brisée (page 24)

lemon filling

4 large eggs, separated

150 g caster sugar

finely grated zest of 2 lemons or 3 limes

freshly squeezed juice of 1 lemon or 2 limes

a pinch of salt

450 g fresh blueberries

confectioners' sugar, to dust

to serve

crème fraîche

extra blueberries

8 tartlet tins, 10 cm diameter

a baking sheet

makes 8 tartlets

Bring the pastry to room temperature. Preheat the oven to 200°C (400°F) Gas 6.

Roll out the pastry on a lightly floured work surface, then use to line the tart tins. Prick the bases and chill or freeze for 15 minutes. Bake blind following the method given on page 19.

Lower the oven to 160°C (325°F) Gas 3. Whisk the egg yolks and 75 g of the sugar with an electric beater until the mixture is pale and mousse-like, and leaves a trail when the beaters are lifted. Whisk in the lemon or lime zest and juice. Set the bowl over a saucepan of simmering water and stir the mixture until thickened enough to coat the back of a wooden spoon. Let cool.

Whisk the egg whites with the salt until soft peaks form, then gradually whisk in the remaining sugar, a spoonful at a time. Beat a spoonful of the egg white mixture into the lemon mixture to loosen it, then carefully fold in the remainder.

Put a single layer of blueberries into each tartlet case. Carefully cover with spoonfuls of the lemon mousse, making sure the mousse seals the edges. Put onto the baking sheet and bake for 15–20 minutes until beginning to rise. Dust with confectioners' sugar and return to the oven for 4–5 minutes until just beginning to brown.

Serve warm (the tartlets will sink a little) or at room temperature with spoonfuls of crème fraîche and extra blueberries.

blueberry and lime sour cream pie

1 recipe Pâte Brisée (page 24)

300 ml sour cream

2 tablespoons freshly squeezed lime juice

2 tablespoons Drambuie or other whisky liqueur

100 g caster sugar

¼ teaspoon ground cinnamon

¼ teaspoon ground allspice

a pinch of salt

2 large eggs, beaten

450 g fresh blueberries

100 ml lime marmalade

a deep tart tin, 22 cm diameter, 3 cm deep

serves 6

The combination of blueberries and lime is terrific, especially when laced with the herby notes of Drambuie. I first tasted wild blueberries sprinkled with Drambuie while fishing in the lochs of Scotland – it was manna from heaven.

Bring the pastry to room temperature. Preheat the oven to 200°C (400°F) Gas 6.

Roll out the pastry thinly on a lightly floured work surface, then use to line the tart tin. Prick the base, then chill or freeze for 15 minutes. Bake blind following the method on page 19.

Lower the oven to 180°C (350°F) Gas 4. Put the sour cream, lime juice, Drambuie or other whisky liqueur, sugar, spices, salt and eggs into a bowl and mix well. Put a single layer of blueberries into the pastry case and pour over the sour cream mixture.

Put the baking sheet into the oven to heat. Bake the tart on the preheated sheet for 45 minutes until the filling is set and the pastry cooked. Remove from the oven and let cool. Remove from the tart tin.

Melt the marmalade and, when runny, strain through a sieve. Mix the rest of the blueberries with the marmalade and pile on top of the cooled pie. Chill for at least 1 hour, but remove from the refrigerator 15 minutes before serving.

strawberry chocolate tarts

I make these for special teatime treats in the summer when Scottish strawberries are in season. They beat anything you can buy from the baker or supermarket. Brushing the inside of the pastry cases with chocolate keeps the pastry crisp and adds a new dimension to the traditional strawberry tart.

1 recipe Sweet Rich Shortcrust Pastry (page 14, see note)

200 g plain chocolate, to make swirls and brush the pastry cases

mascarpone filling

250 g mascarpone cheese

2 tablespoons caster sugar

250 g fromage frais or curd cheese

rosewater or Grand Marnier, to taste

strawberry topping

12 large, ripe strawberries

redcurrant jelly, for brushing

a biscuit cutter, 10 cm diameter

12 deep fluted tart or brioche tins, 8 cm diameter

non-stick baking parchment

makes 12 small deep tarts

Bring the pastry to room temperature. Preheat the oven to 190°C (375°F) Gas 5.

Roll out the pastry as thinly as possible on a lightly floured work surface, then cut out 12 circles with the biscuit cutter. Use these to line 6 of the tart or brioche tins.

Trim the edges and prick the bases. Then set another tin inside each one – this will weight down the pastry while it is baking. Chill or freeze for 15 minutes. Bake blind for 10–12 minutes until golden and set. Remove the inner tins and return to the oven to dry out for 5 minutes. Cool, then remove from the outer tins. Repeat with the remaining pastry to make another 6.

Melt the chocolate and sprinkle spoonfuls randomly from a height onto non-stick baking parchment. Let cool until set. Use the remaining chocolate to brush the insides of the tarts, making sure they are completely covered. Let cool and set.

To make the filling, put the mascarpone and sugar into a bowl and beat until creamy, then beat in the fromage frais or curd cheese. Add rosewater or Grand Marnier to taste.

Spoon this mixture into the tartlets, filling well, then sit a nice fat strawberry on top. Melt the redcurrant jelly, cool slightly, then brush over the strawberries and the exposed mascarpone surface. Set aside in a cool place to set.

To serve, break up the set chocolate swirls and push a shard into each tart. Serve immediately.

Really ripe strawberries nestling on top of a vanilla pastry cream scented with orange flower water and smothered in redcurrant jelly – the taste of summer in a tart! Pâte sucrée is the ideal pastry here, since it bakes to a sweet crispness and doesn't go soggy. Rather than using melted redcurrant jelly for the glaze, I've made a strawberry sauce with gelatine, which will stay set for some time.

classic strawberry vanilla tart

1 recipe Pâte Sucrée (page 26)

vanilla crème pâtissière

4 egg yolks

75 g caster sugar

25 g all-purpose flour

1 vanilla pod

300 ml milk

2 tablespoons orange flower water
or kirsch

strawberry glaze

75 g strawberries, sliced

1 tablespoon caster sugar

5 tablespoons water

$1/2$ teaspoon powdered gelatine

to serve

450 g evenly sized ripe strawberries

*a loose-based rectangular tart tin,
24 x 11.5 cm, or a round loose-based
tart tin, 24 cm diameter*

serves 6

Bring the pastry to room temperature. Preheat the oven to 190°C (375°F) Gas 5.

Roll out the pastry thinly on a lightly floured work surface, then use to line the tart tin. Prick the base, then chill or freeze for 15 minutes.

Line with foil and baking beans and bake blind for 15 minutes. Remove the foil and beans, turn the oven down to 180°C (350°F) Gas 4 and return to the oven for 10–15 minutes to dry out and brown. Let cool, then remove from the tin and set on the serving platter.

Meanwhile, to make the crème pâtissière, put the egg yolks and sugar into a bowl and beat until pale and thick. Beat in the flour. Cut the vanilla pod in half lengthways and scrape out the tiny black seeds. Whisk the seeds into the milk, bring to the boil, then pour onto the egg mixture, whisking all the time. Return to the pan and slowly bring to the boil, stirring constantly. Cook gently for 2–3 minutes (it doesn't matter if it boils), then beat in the orange flower water or kirsch and pour into the pastry case. Level the surface and let cool completely.

To make the strawberry glaze, put the 75 g sliced strawberries, sugar and 5 tablespoons water into a small saucepan and simmer for 5 minutes until soft. Blend or sieve to give a purée. Sprinkle the gelatine over 2 tablespoons water in a small bowl. Heat the bowl until the gelatine has dissolved, then stir into the purée. Let cool until just beginning to set and thicken.

While the glaze is cooling, slice the 450 g strawberries finely and arrange over the surface of the cold vanilla cream. Spoon or brush the cooled glaze over the strawberries and chill for at least I hour to set. Serve cool, but not refrigerator cold.

A tart that celebrates the perfect marriage of raspberries and cream. This is simplicity itself to make, but must be assembled at the last moment to keep the freshness and crispness of the pastry. I like to sweeten the cream with a little sieved homemade raspberry jam and I add a dash of framboise (raspberry liqueur) if I have it.

fresh raspberry tart

1 recipe Pâte Brisée (page 24)

2–3 tablespoons homemade raspberry jam

600 ml double cream, or 300 ml double cream mixed with 300 ml crème fraîche

2 tablespoons framboise, (optional)

750 g fresh raspberries

150 ml raspberry or redcurrant jelly (any berry jelly will do)

a loose-based fluted tart tin, 20.5 cm diameter

serves 6–8

Bring the pastry to room temperature. Preheat the oven to 200°C (400°F) Gas 6.

Roll out the pastry thinly on a lightly floured work surface, and use to line the tart tin. Prick the base, chill or freeze for 15 minutes. then bake blind following the method given on page 19. Leave to cool.*

Press the raspberry jam through a sieve to remove the seeds, then put into a large bowl. Add the cream and framboise if using. Whisk until thick and just holding peaks. Spoon into the tart case and level the surface. Cover with the raspberries, arranging a final neat layer on top.

Put the raspberry or redcurrant jelly into a small saucepan and warm it gently until liquid. Brush over the raspberries to glaze. Put into the refrigerator to chill and set for 10 minutes only before serving (no longer or the tart will go soggy).

*Note You may like to brush the inside of the tart shell with melted white chocolate before filling – this will keep the pastry crisp, and make the tart even more of a special treat! You could also decorate the top with white chocolate curls (use a chocolate with a low cocoa solid content, bring it to room temperature first, then shave with a potato peeler).

Variation I sometimes lightly toss the raspberries in the jelly (you may need a bit extra jelly to do this), coating them completely without breaking them. I then spoon them over the surface in a higgledy-piggledy fashion.

Another French pâtisserie classic. The secret of this tart is patience and neatness because it just has to look beautiful! Make it with the juiciest apples you can – Golden Delicious are very good. The pastry provides a firm, crisp support. Unsweetened Pâte Brisée is used here, because the tart has to be baked for a long time and pastries with a high sugar content would scorch before the apples were cooked.

tarte aux pommes
(French apple tart)

1 recipe Pâte Brisée (page 24)

apple filling

4–5 well-flavoured dessert apples, peeled and cored

3 tablespoons caster sugar

50 g unsalted butter, cubed

4–6 tablespoons apricot jam

2 tablespoons Calvados (apple brandy) or brandy

a loose-based tart tin, 25 cm diameter

a baking sheet

serves 6–8

Bring the pastry to room temperature. Preheat the oven to 200°C (400°F) Gas 6 and put a baking sheet in the oven to heat.

Roll out thinly on a lightly floured work surface and use to line the tart tin. Chill or freeze for 15 minutes.

Meanwhile, slice the apples thinly, and coarsely chop up the uneven smaller pieces. Arrange these smaller pieces in the base of the tart. Cover with one-third of the slices any way you like. Arrange the remaining slices neatly in concentric rings over the chopped apples. Sprinkle with the sugar and dot with the butter.

Set the tart tin on the baking sheet and bake at for about 1 hour until the apples are very well browned and the pastry golden. Remove from the oven and transfer to a cooling rack. Wait for 5 minutes, then remove the tart tin.

Put the apricot jam and Calvados into a small saucepan and warm gently. Strain, then use to glaze the apples. Serve at room temperature.

This familiar favourite is easy to make – and a must for anyone with a young family. The fruit filling is not too spicy, and children will love the crumble topping.

lemony apple crumble tart

1 recipe Basic Shortcrust Pastry (page 13) or Sweet Rich Shortcrust Pastry (page 14, see note)

custard, to serve

crumble topping

75 g all-purpose flour

75 g demerara sugar

75 g unsalted butter, softened

finely grated zest of 1 unwaxed lemon

spiced apple filling

6 large Cox's Orange Pippins or Granny Smiths, peeled and cored

55 g sultanas

finely grated zest and juice of 1 unwaxed lemon

55 g soft brown sugar

½ teaspoon cinnamon

¼ teaspoon nutmeg

1 tablespoon each all-purpose flour and caster sugar, mixed

a tart tin, 23 cm diameter

serves 6

Bring the pastry to room temperature. Preheat the oven to 200°C (400°F) Gas 6, or 190°C (375°F) Gas 5 if using Sweet Rich Shortcrust Pastry.

Roll out the pastry on a lightly floured work surface, and use to line the tart tin. Prick the base, then chill or freeze for 15 minutes. Bake blind following the method given on page 19. Let cool.

To make the topping, put the flour, sugar, butter and lemon zest into a bowl and rub lightly between your fingers until the mixture resembles fine breadcrumbs. Chill in the refrigerator until needed.

To make the apple filling, chop the apples into small chunks, put into a bowl and toss with the sultanas, lemon zest and juice, sugar and spices. Sprinkle the base of the pastry case with the flour and caster sugar, then arrange the apples on top.

Sprinkle the crumble mixture over the apples. Bake for 15 minutes, then reduce the temperature to 180°C (350°F) Gas 4 and bake for another 30 minutes. Serve warm with custard.

A tart named after the sisters who, as legend has it, created an upside-down apple tart by mistake! The type of apple used is crucial here – it must retain its shape during cooking and yet have a good flavour. I like to use Cox's Orange Pippins, Golden Delicious or Jonagolds.

tarte des demoiselles tatin

1 recipe Rough Puff Pastry (page 35) or Cheat's Rough Puff Pastry (page 39) or 450 g frozen puff pastry, thawed

300 g granulated sugar

150 g chilled unsalted butter, thinly sliced

2¼–2½ kg evenly sized dessert apples

crème fraîche or whipped cream, to serve

non-stick baking parchment

a baking sheet

a flameproof cast-iron frying pan or tarte tatin dish, 28 cm diameter

serves 6

Preheat the oven to 190°C (375°F) Gas 5.

Roll out the pastry on non-stick baking parchment to a circle about 30 cm in diameter, slide onto a baking sheet and chill. Sprinkle the sugar over the base of the frying pan or tarte tatin dish. Cover with the sliced butter.

Peel, halve and core the apples. Add the apple halves to the outside edge of the pan – set the first one at an angle, almost on its edge, then arrange the others all around the edge so that they slightly overlap and butt up against each other. Add another ring of apples inside, so that the pan is almost filled, then put a whole half to fill the gap in the centre. The apples should now cover the entire surface of the pan. They look awkward and bulky, but will cook down and meld together later.

Put the pan over gentle heat and cook for about 45 minutes until the sugar and butter have caramelized and the apples have softened underneath. (Check from time to time and adjust the heat if necessary. The juices will gradually bubble up the sides; keep cooking until they are a dark amber.)

Lay the pastry over the apples in the pan and tuck the edges down into the pan, making the rim of the tart. Prick the top of the pastry here and there with a fork, then set the pan on the baking sheet. Bake in the preheated oven for 25–30 minutes until the pastry is risen and golden.

Remove the pan from the oven and immediately invert the tart onto a warm serving plate (watch out for hot caramel). Replace any apple slices that stick to the pan. Serve warm, not hot, with crème fraîche or whipped cream.

What could be better than the simplicity of pears poached in red wine? This tart is! The pears absorb the deep flavour of the wine and turn a fabulously rich colour. If you want to be outrageously extravagant, use Italian Vin Santo or Marsala instead of wine and cut down on the sugar – the pears will turn a beautiful dark mahogany.

drunken pear tart

1 recipe Pâte Brisée (page 24) or Cheat's Rough Puff Pastry (page 39)

8 under-ripe medium pears

1 cinnamon stick

75 g caster sugar

600 ml full-bodied red wine

slivered pistachios or almonds, to finish

crème fraîche or whipped cream, to serve

a cast-iron frying pan, 25 cm diameter

serves 6

If using Pâte Brisée, bring to room temperature before rolling out.

Peel the pears, halve lengthways and carefully scoop out the core with a teaspoon or melon baller. Arrange them around the base of the frying pan in concentric circles, wide ends outwards and the points facing into the centre. Any pears remaining should be cut up and used to fill any gaps.

Crumble the cinnamon over the top and sprinkle with the sugar. Carefully pour in the red wine, then bring to the boil. Cover and simmer gently for about 1 hour or until tender.

Preheat the oven to 200°C (400°F) Gas 6. Uncover the pan and hold a plate or pan lid over the pears to hold them back while you pour off the juices into a saucepan. Boil the juices hard until well reduced and syrupy, then sprinkle back over the pears.

Roll out the dough on a lightly floured work surface to a circle slightly larger than the diameter of the pan. Lift the pastry over the pears and tuck the edge of the pastry down into the pan. Bake for about 35–40 minutes until the pastry is crisp and golden.

As soon as it is ready, invert the tart onto a plate or it will stick – the fruit will be very hot, so be careful you don't burn your fingers. Serve warm or at room temperature, sprinkled with the pistachios or almonds and a good deal of crème fraîche or whipped cream.

free-form caramelized peach tart

1 recipe Puff Pastry (page 29),
Rough Puff Pastry (page 35)
or Cheat's Rough Puff Pastry (page 39)

4–6 ripe peaches

55 g butter

freshly squeezed juice of ½ lemon

150 g caster sugar

whipped cream or crème fraîche, to serve

*a dinner plate, 28 cm diameter
(to use as a template)*

a baking sheet

serves 6

The original version of this tart is sold at my local pâtisserie in France. Monsieur Demont makes all his own pastry on the premises, and when peaches are in season and at their best, these tarts appear in the window in all their rustic glory. So simple and so good – especially with all-butter homemade pastry.

Preheat the oven to 230°C (450°F) Gas 8.

Roll out the pastry on a lightly floured work surface and cut out a circle, 28 cm diameter, using a large dinner plate as a template. Lift onto a baking sheet and make an edge by twisting the pastry over itself all the way around the edge. Press lightly to seal. Still on the baking sheet, chill or freeze for at least 15 minutes.

Peel the peaches if necessary, then halve and pit them and cut into chunky slices. Put the butter into a saucepan, then add the lemon juice and half the sugar. Heat until melted, then add the peaches and toss gently. Pile the peaches all over the pastry in a casual way. Sprinkle with the remaining sugar and bake in the preheated oven for 20–25 minutes until golden, puffed and caramelized. Serve with whipped cream or crème fraîche.

A classic of the French pâtisserie – thin crisp pastry filled with a thin layer of golden custard and topped with soft, musky apricots, glistening with apricot jam and their edges just 'caught' in the oven. The tart shell is not baked blind beforehand because it would burn.

tarte aux abricots (apricot tart)

1 recipe Pâte Sucrée (page 26) or My Just-Push-It-In Pastry (page 41)

crème pâtissière

5 medium egg yolks

75 g caster sugar

3 tablespoons all-purpose flour

400 ml milk

2 tablespoons kirsch or brandy

apricot topping and glaze

500–600 g fresh apricots, depending on their size

50 g caster sugar

3 tablespoons apricot jam, to glaze

a little kirsch or brandy

a loose-based tart tin, 25 cm diameter

a non-stick baking sheet with a rim

a regular baking sheet

a wire rack

serves 6–8

If using Pâte Sucrée, bring to room temperature before rolling out.

To make the crème pâtissière, put the egg yolks and sugar into a bowl and beat until pale and thick. Beat in the flour. Put the milk into a small saucepan and bring to the boil, then whisk into the egg mixture. Return the mixture to the pan and bring to the boil again, stirring constantly. Cook gently for 2–3 minutes. then pour into a bowl and let cool, covering the surface with clingfilm to prevent a skin from forming.

Roll out the Pâte Sucrée, if using, and line the tart tin. Alternatively, line the tin with My Just-Push-It-In Pastry rounds. Chill for at least 30 minutes.

Preheat the oven to 230°C (450°F) Gas 8 (or as hot as the oven will go).

Cut the apricots in half and remove the pits. Arrange them cut side down on the baking sheet and sprinkle with sugar. Bake for 5 minutes until softening and beginning to release their juices. Drain off and reserve the juices.

Lower the oven to 200°C (400°F) Gas 6 and put the baking sheet on the middle shelf to preheat. Beat the 2 tablespoons kirsch into the cooled crème pâtissière and spread over the base of the pastry case. Arrange the apricots closely together, cut side up, over the crème. Set the tart tin on the preheated baking sheet and bake for about 40 minutes, until the apricots colour and the tart is a deep golden brown.* Cool for 10 minutes before lifting off the outer ring and transferring to the wire rack to cool completely.

Put the apricot jam into a small saucepan, add the reserved apricot juice and kirsch or brandy to taste, and heat gently until liquid. Strain, then use to glaze the tart. Serve at room temperature, preferably on the day of making.

*Note This tart is not baked blind, but setting the tart tin on a preheated baking sheet will help to ensure that the base cooks quickly and goes crisp.

The rich buttery brioche pastry contains a set golden custard studded with fresh cherries. This is one of those moreish pastries best served in thin slices with a cup of tea or coffee.

golden custard and cherry brioche tart

brioche pastry

2 teaspoons active dried yeast*

4 tablespoons milk, warmed

15 g caster sugar

250 g strong all-purpose flour

1 teaspoon salt

2 large eggs, at room temperature

180 g unsalted butter, softened

custard and cherry filling

200 ml milk

100 ml double cream

1 vanilla pod

2 large eggs, plus 1 egg yolk

125 g caster or vanilla sugar

3 tablespoons all-purpose flour

350 g fresh cherries, pitted

extra beaten egg, to glaze

a rectangular loose-based tart tin, 33 x 9.5 cm

serves 6

*To use easy-blend dried yeast, mix 1 teaspoon in with the dry ingredients, then add the eggs and finish as in the main recipe.

To make the pastry, dissolve the yeast in the warm milk with a pinch of the sugar. Cover and leave in a warm place for 10 minutes to froth.

Sift the flour into a bowl with the remaining sugar and the salt. Put the eggs into a bowl, whisk well, then make a well in the flour and pour in the eggs and the frothy yeast mixture. Mix to a soft elastic dough. Add a little more flour if necessary, but keep the dough quite soft. Work in the softened butter until smooth, shiny and elastic. The dough will not form a ball at this stage. (If preferred, the whole process can be done easily in a large electric food mixer using the 'K' beater.)

Cover and let rise in a warm place for 2–4 hours until doubled in size (or leave overnight in the refrigerator). Knock back, then wrap and chill until firm enough to roll out – this takes about 30 minutes.

To make the custard, put the milk, cream and split vanilla pod into a saucepan and heat until until almost boiling. Leave to infuse for 15 minutes. Beat the eggs, egg yolk and sugar together until pale and creamy. Remove the vanilla pod from the milk and cream mixture.** Beat the flour into the egg mixture, then whisk in the milk and cream mixture. Set aside.

Preheat the oven to 200°C (400°F) Gas 6. Roll out the remaining pastry and use to line the tart tin. Pour in the custard, dot with the cherries and leave in a warm place to rise for 20 minutes. Bake for 15–20 minutes or until the custard is just starting to set.

Turn the oven down to 160°C (325°F) Gas 3. Brush the pastry edges with the beaten egg and bake for a further 45 minutes until golden and set. Cool in the tin. Serve at room temperature.

****Note** Wash and dry the pod, then put into a sugar jar to make vanilla sugar.

Open jam tarts are made wherever there is a tradition of jam-making – but this one is surely the Queen of Jam Tarts! Use the very best homemade jam you can find – that's what will make this tart. If the hazelnuts are not ground finely enough, grind them in a blender together with the sugar to prevent them from sticking.

linzertorte

(Austrian and German jam tart)

hazelnut pastry

200 g all-purpose flour
½ teaspoon ground cinnamon
½ teaspoon mixed spice
1 teaspoon cocoa powder
200 g unsalted butter, chilled
200 g very finely ground hazelnuts
200 g caster sugar
1 egg, beaten
2 tablespoons kirsch

to fill and finish

250 g top quality raspberry jam
1 egg yolk, beaten, to glaze
confectioners' sugar, to dust (optional)

*a plate, 20 cm diameter
(to use as a template)*
a plain tart tin, 24 cm diameter
a baking sheet
non-stick baking parchment

serves 6

Preheat the oven to 200°C (400°F) Gas 6.

Sift all the dry ingredients for the pastry into a bowl. Rub in the butter until it resembles fine breadcrumbs. Stir in the hazelnuts and sugar, beaten egg and kirsch. Bring together first with round-bladed knife, then with your hands. Knead lightly into a ball and divide in 2 unequal pieces comprising one-third and two-thirds of the pastry. Flatten each slightly and wrap in clingfilm. Chill in the refrigerator for at least 30 minutes.

Roll out the smaller piece of pastry on non-stick baking parchment. Cut a circle the same diameter as the 24 cm tart tin, then cut out a 20 cm inner circle, using the plate as a guide, to give a band about 2 cm wide. Cut 6 more strips of pastry 2 cm wide and 24 cm long (you can use a fluted pastry wheel for this). Chill in the refrigerator.

Roll out the larger piece of pastry and use to line the base and sides of the tart tin set on the baking sheet. Prick the base all over with a fork. Spread the jam evenly over the base, leaving the edge clear. Then flip the edge of the pastry carefully over the jam to form a tiny edge or rim (trim as necessary), as shown on page 22. Freeze for 15 minutes if the pastry is getting very soft.

Brush the rim of the tart base with a little water and set the 6 pastry strips in a lattice pattern over the jam. Brush the edges with a little more water, then lay the circular band on top, gently press to seal and trim where necessary.

Brush the pastry top with the beaten egg and bake for about 20 minutes or until firm and golden. Cool and remove from the tin. Fill up any deep holes with more jam, and serve at room temperature, dusted with confectioners' sugar, if using. The linzertorte may be kept in an airtight container for up to 2 weeks.

cranberry cinnamon crunch tart

streusel pastry

250 g butter, softened

50 g caster sugar

2 tablespoons sunflower oil

1 teaspoon real vanilla essence

1 medium egg

450 g all-purpose flour

1 teaspoon baking powder

¼ teaspoon salt

2 teaspoons ground cinnamon

cranberry sauce

350 g fresh or frozen cranberries

125 g caster sugar

grated zest and juice of 1 orange

to finish

75 g demerara sugar

confectioners' sugar, to dust

a springform cake tin, 25 cm diameter

non-stick baking parchment

serves 12

A delightful cross between a biscuit and a cake. The light almost shortbread pastry has a layer of thick cranberry sauce in the middle, providing a sharp contrast to its butteriness. Delicious cut into thin wedges and served with coffee.

To make the cranberry sauce, put the cranberries and sugar into a food processor and chop coarsely. Transfer to saucepan and add the orange zest and juice. Bring to the boil, stirring constantly. Simmer for 5 minutes, then set aside to cool completely.

To make the streusel pastry, cream the butter and sugar in a bowl until light and fluffy. Beat in the sunflower oil and vanilla essence. Lightly whisk the egg and beat into the mixture. Sift the flour, baking powder, salt and spice together into a second bowl bowl. Gradually stir into the first bowl until the dough resembles a coarse shortbread mixture. Bring the dough together with your hands and knead lightly into a ball. Wrap and chill for at least 2 hours or until very firm.

Line the base of the cake tin with the non-stick baking parchment. Butter and flour the sides of the tin. When the dough is thoroughly chilled, remove from the refrigerator and unwrap. Divide into 2 and return the piece you are not using immediately to the refrigerator.

Grate the first half of the dough coarsely into the tin to cover the base evenly. Do not pack down. Carefully spoon in the cold cranberry sauce, avoiding the edges. Remove the remaining dough from the refrigerator and grate evenly over the top, then sprinkle thickly with the demerara sugar. Bake at 150°C (300°F) Gas 2 for about 1¼–1½ hours until pale but firm.

Cool in the tin, then unclip and remove the tart from the tin. Dust with confectioners' sugar to serve. The tart may be stored in an airtight container for up to 1 week.

Fresh dates are so sweet and sticky, they make a fantastic quick-and-easy topping for a crisp puff pastry base. The maple syrup and sugar caramelize with the butter and give the tarts a wonderful sheen. Don't serve them too hot, or you will burn your mouth.

sticky date flaky tarts
with caramel oranges

1 recipe Puff Pastry (page 29),
Rough Puff Pastry (page 35)
or Cheat's Rough Puff Pastry (page 39)

caramel oranges

4 small, juicy, thin-skinned oranges

125 g sugar

date topping

55 g butter

30 g soft light brown sugar

2 tablespoons maple syrup

12–16 fresh Medjool dates

75 g walnut pieces

*a saucer or similar, 13 cm diameter
(to use as a template)*

a large baking sheet

serves 4

Preheat the oven to 200°C (400°F) Gas 6.

Roll out the pastry thinly on a lightly floured work surface, then cut out 4 circles, 13 cm diameter, using the saucer as a guide. Put these onto a large baking sheet, prick all over, then chill or freeze for 15 minutes.

To make the caramel oranges, slice the top and bottom off each orange, then cut off the skin in a spiral, as if you were peeling an apple. Try to remove all the bitter white pith. Slice down between the membranes and flick out each segment. Catch the juice in a bowl, then squeeze the remaining juice out of the membrane 'skeletons'.

Put the sugar and 3 tablespoons water into a heavy-based saucepan. Put over low heat until the sugar has completely dissolved and the liquid is clear. Increase the heat and boil until the liquid turns a dark caramel colour. Quickly remove the pan from the heat, stand back and add another 3 tablespoons water – it will hiss and splutter.

Return the pan to a low heat, and stir until all the hardened pieces of caramel have dissolved. Pour in the reserved orange juice and boil hard until very thick and syrupy. Remove from the heat and let cool completely before adding the orange segments. Chill until needed.

To make the date topping, cut the dates in half and remove the pits. Put the butter, sugar and maple syrup in a saucepan and melt over gentle heat, then add the dates and walnuts.

Spoon the mixture over the circles, leaving a small clear rim on the outside of each. Bake for 15–18 minutes until the pastry is risen and golden and the dates sizzling. Serve with the caramel oranges.

My grandmother made wonderful tartlets in bun trays and let me fill them with bright yellow shop-bought lemon curd.
I don't know if she would approve of these exotic mouthfuls – they are very wicked. Remember, the more wrinkled the passionfruit, the riper the flesh inside. Why not make double the quantity of curd and pot up any you don't use?

pineapple and passionfruit curd tartlets

1 recipe Pâte Sucrée (page 26)

passionfruit curd

6 ripe, juicy passionfruit

freshly squeezed juice of 1 small lemon, strained

75 g butter, cubed

3 large eggs, beaten

225 g sugar

fruit topping

1 small fresh pineapple, peeled, cored and sliced

4 passionfruit

a fluted biscuit cutter, 7.5 cm diameter

a 12-hole bun tray

makes 12 tartlets

Bring the pastry to room temperature before rolling out.

Cut the 6 passionfruit in half, scoop out the flesh and press through a sieve into a medium bowl to extract the juice. Add the lemon juice, butter, eggs and sugar and set over a saucepan of simmering water (or cook in a double boiler). Cook, stirring all the time, for about 20 minutes or until the curd has thickened considerably. If you are brave enough, you can cook this over direct heat, watching that it doesn't get too hot and curdle. Strain into a bowl and set aside.

Preheat the oven to 180°C (350°F) Gas 4. Roll out the pastry thinly on a lightly floured work surface and cut out 12 rounds with the biscuit cutter. Line the bun tray with the pastry, pressing it into the holes. Prick the bases and chill or freeze for 15 minutes. Bake blind for 5–6 minutes without lining with beans. Let cool.

When ready to serve, fill the tartlet cases with a spoonful of passionfruit curd, then top with sliced pineapple. Cut the 4 passionfruit in half, scoop out the flesh and spoon a little, seeds and all, over each tartlet. Serve immediately before the tartlets have a chance to go soggy.

This is an outrage of a tart! Clouds of gooey pavlova meringue float on top of a luscious filling of sliced fresh mango. Lime is the natural partner for mango, enhancing the wonderful exotic taste.

mango pavlova tart with lime sauce

1 recipe Pâte Brisée (page 24) or Pâte Sucrée (page 26)

1 egg, beaten, to glaze

1 tablespoon flour mixed with 1 tablespoon sugar

2–3 ripe mangoes, peeled

pavlova topping

4 large egg whites

a pinch of salt

225 g caster sugar

1 teaspoon cornflour

1 teaspoon vanilla essence

1 teaspoon vinegar

lime sauce

finely grated zest and juice of 3 large unwaxed limes

2 tablespoons dark rum

55–75 g sugar, to taste

a deep tart tin, 23 cm diameter

serves 6

Bring the pastry to room temperature. Preheat the oven to 200°C (400°F) Gas 6 if using Pâte Brisée, and 190°C (375°F) Gas 5 if using Pâte Sucrée.

Roll out the pastry thinly on a lightly floured work surface, then use to line the tart tin. Prick with a fork, then chill or freeze for 15 minutes.

If using Pâte Brisée, bake blind following the method given on page 19. If using Pâte Sucrée, line with foil or all-purpose clingfilm and baking beans, then bake blind for 15 minutes. Remove the foil and beans, turn the oven down to 180°C (350°F) Gas 4 and return to the oven for 10–15 minutes to dry out and brown.

Brush the inside of the tart with the beaten egg and return to the oven for 5–10 minutes until the egg glaze has cooked. Brush and bake again if necessary. Let cool, then sprinkle with the flour and sugar mixture. Lower the oven temperature to 140°C (275°F) Gas 1.

Cut the mangoes down each side of the stone and slice the flesh. Arrange the mango slices over the base of the tart.

To make the pavlova topping, put the egg whites and salt into a bowl and whisk until very stiff. Gradually whisk in the caster sugar, one large spoonful at a time – making sure that the meringue is 'bouncily' stiff before adding the next spoonful. Whisk in the cornflour, vanilla and vinegar.

Spoon the meringue mixture over the tart, making sure that you seal the edges. Pile the mixture as high as you can. Bake for about 45 minutes until just turning palest brown.

While the tart is cooking, make the lime sauce. Put the lime zest and juice, rum and sugar into a small saucepan and heat until the sugar melts. Boil for 1 minute, then pour into a jug and let cool.

Remove the tart from the oven, cool slightly, then serve with the lime sauce.

My Scottish-Canadian cousin, Deirdre, introduced us to this pie when living with us in Scotland for a while, back in the 1960s. It seemed so exotic in the far north of Britain – none of us having even seen a pumpkin before, never mind cans of purée – and has remained a family favourite ever since. Butternut squash purée makes an acceptable substitute if pumpkin is not available.

pumpkin pie

1 recipe American Pie Crust (page 16)

pumpkin filling

500 ml homemade pumpkin purée or one 475 g can*

100 g light soft brown sugar

3 large eggs

200 ml evaporated milk

120 ml golden syrup

a good pinch of salt

1 teaspoon cinnamon

½ teaspoon mixed spice

1 teaspoon real vanilla essence

2 tablespoons rum (optional)

2 tart tins or pie plates, 22 cm diameter

makes two 22 cm pies

*To make the purée, cut a pumpkin or butternut squash into large chunks and bake for about 1 hour at 160°C (325°F) Gas 3. Scrape the flesh from the skin and purée until smooth in a food processor.

Bring the pastry to room temperature. Preheat the oven to 190°C (375°F) Gas 5.

Roll out the pastry thinly on a lightly floured work surface, then use to line the 2 tart tins or pie plates. Trim and crimp or decorate the edges as you wish (see page 23). Prick the bases all over with a fork, chill or freeze for 15 minutes, then bake blind following the method given on page 19.

Lower the oven to 160°C (325°F) Gas 3.

Put all the filling ingredients into a food processor and blend until smooth. Pour into the pastry cases, set on a baking sheet and bake for about 1 hour or until just set. Remove from the oven and let stand for 10 minutes, then remove the tart tin and let cool for a few minutes. Serve warm or at room temperature, not chilled.

Treacle tart in England is made with golden syrup, white breadcrumbs and lemon juice. In Scotland, we use real black treacle in lots of our baking, so I have adapted this tart to be made with proper treacle as well as pumpernickel (German rye bread) breadcrumbs and lime juice. The pumpernickel gives it an unusual, wonderful texture. The bananas just have to be there!

real treacle tart
with caramelized bananas

½ recipe Sweet Rich Shortcrust Pastry
(page 14, see note)*

5 tablespoons treacle

5 tablespoons golden syrup

finely grated zest and juice
of 1 large unwaxed lime

½ teaspoon freshly grated ginger
(optional but recommended)

100 g pumpernickel crumbs (use a food
processor to make the crumbs)

caramelized bananas

2 large bananas

55 g unsalted butter

3 tablespoons demerara sugar

a squeeze of fresh lemon juice

custard, clotted cream or crème fraîche,
to serve

a pie plate, 20 cm diameter

serves 4–6

*Make the full recipe, then freeze the
remainder for later use.*

Bring the pastry to room temperature. Preheat the oven to 190°C (375°F) Gas 5.

On a lightly floured work surface, roll out the pastry to a thickness of 5 mm. Use to line the pie plate and prick the base. Make a traditional decorative edge following the method given for the devil edge on page 23. Chill or freeze the pastry for 15 minutes.

Put the treacle and golden syrup into a saucepan, add the lime juice and zest and ginger, if using, and heat until just warm and runny. Stir the pumpernickel crumbs. Spread into the pastry case and bake for about 30 minutes or until the filling is just set and the pastry is browning at the edges.**

Meanwhile, peel and cut the bananas into chunks. Melt the butter in a frying pan and add the sugar. Cook for a couple of minutes until the sugar melts, then turn up the heat and cook until it caramelizes. Add the bananas and toss well to coat with the juices. Fry over a medium heat until starting to colour and smelling delicious. Squeeze in some lemon juice, and remove from the heat.

Cool the tart slightly before serving warm with the bananas and custard, clotted cream or crème fraîche.

Note Because the tart is not baked blind, slipping it onto a preheated baking sheet will help to make the base cook quickly and crisply.

There's nothing quite as delicious as a real custard tart. I come from a long line of bakers, and these would be one of our 'desert island' luxuries. The nutmeg is the classic flavouring here, but I infuse the milk with fresh bay leaf to add a mysterious musky scent to the custard. Fresh bay leaves should be more widely used in cooking – the flavour is like nutmeg, but 'greener' and sweeter.

little nutmeg and bay leaf custard tarts

1 recipe Pâte Sucrée (page 26)*

nutmeg and bay leaf custard

600 ml full-cream milk

3 fresh (preferably) or dried bay leaves

6 egg yolks

75 g caster sugar

1 whole nutmeg

8 loose-based tart tins, 10 cm diameter (or use smaller but deeper tins and increase the cooking time)

2 baking sheets

a wire rack

makes about 8 tarts

*Use any leftover pastry to make a few more tarts.

Bring the pastry to room temperature. Preheat the oven to 200°C (400°F) Gas 6.

Roll out the pastry thinly on a lightly floured work surface and use to line the tart tins. Put these on the baking sheet and chill for 30 minutes.

To make the custard, put the milk and bay leaves into a saucepan and heat until lukewarm. Put the egg yolks and sugar into a bowl and beat until pale and creamy. Pour the warmed milk onto the yolks and stir well – do not whisk or you will get bubbles. Strain into a jug and pour into the tart cases. Grate fresh nutmeg liberally over the surface of the tartlets.

Preheat the other baking sheet in the oven.** Put the tart tins onto the preheated sheet and bake in the oven for 10 minutes. Lower the heat to 180°C (350°F) Gas 4 and bake until set and just golden – about another 10 minutes. Don't overbake as the custard should be a bit wobbly when the tarts come out of the oven.

Remove from the tins and let cool on a wire rack. Serve at room temperature.

**Note Because the tarts are not baked blind, slipping them onto a preheated baking sheet will help to make the bases cook quickly and crisply.

jacks' rose petal tart

This is the most beautiful and delicious tart in the world. The recipe was given to me by my sister Jacks. It tastes so delicate – and is lovely to serve at a wedding or christening.

1 recipe Puff Pastry (page 29) or 350 g frozen puff pastry, thawed*

rose-flavoured filling

150 ml Greek yoghurt

1 egg yolk

2–3 tablespoons rosewater

2 tablespoons caster sugar

300 ml double cream

crystallized rose petals

1 egg white

caster sugar

petals of 2–4 scented roses

a round or heart-shaped tart tin, 25 cm diameter

foil and baking beans

a wire rack or non-stick baking parchment

makes one 25 cm tart

If using 1 recipe of homemade Puff Pastry, you will have some left over to freeze for later use.

To crystallize the rose petals, put the egg white into a bowl, beat until frothy, then paint onto clean dry petals. Sprinkle with caster sugar to coat completely, then arrange on a cake rack or non-stick baking parchment and leave in a warm place to dry out and crisp – at least overnight. Cool, but do NOT put into the refrigerator. Store between layers of kitchen paper in an airtight container.

Preheat the oven to 230°C (450°F) Gas 8. Roll out the pastry as thinly as possible. Use to line the tart tin, pressing it into the sides and trimming to leave 5 mm hanging over the edge. Turn this inwards to make a rim. Prick the base all over with a fork, then chill or freeze for 15 minutes. Line with foil and baking beans and bake blind for 12–15 minutes. Lower the oven to 200°C (400°F) Gas 6, remove the foil and beans and return to the oven for a further 5 minutes to dry out. You may have to flatten the pastry if it puffs up.

Turn the oven down to 180°C (350°F) Gas 4. Put the yoghurt, egg yolk, rosewater and sugar into a bowl and mix well. Put the cream into a bowl and whisk until soft peaks form, then fold into the yoghurt mixture. Spoon into the baked pastry case, level the surface and bake for about 20 minutes. It will seem almost runny, but will set as it cools. Cover and chill until firm.

Decorate with the crystallized rose petals. Serve slightly cold.

This is wickedly delicious. Use the darkest chocolate you can find and serve in thin slices. The filling is gooey and rich inside – delicious with a spoonful of sour cherry jam and another of crème fraîche. I sometimes spread the base of the tart with the jam before pouring in the mixture.

baked darkest chocolate mousse tart

1 recipe Pâte Sucrée (page 26)

chocolate mousse filling

400 g plain chocolate (60–70 per cent cocoa solids), broken into pieces

125 g unsalted butter, cubed

5 large eggs, separated

125 g caster sugar

150 ml double cream, at room temperature

3 tablespoons dark rum (optional)

to finish

confectioners' sugar, to dust

light cream, to serve

a deep loose-based tart tin, 25 cm diameter, 4 cm deep

foil and baking beans

serves 8

Bring the pastry to room temperature. Preheat the oven to 190°C (375°F) Gas 5.

Roll out the pastry thinly on a lightly floured work surface, then use to line the tart tin. Prick the base, then chill or freeze for 15 minutes.

Line with foil and baking beans and bake blind for 15 minutes. Remove the foil and beans, turn the oven down to 180°C (350°F) Gas 4 and return to the oven for 10–15 minutes to dry out and brown. Cool and remove from the tin, then transfer to a serving platter.

Put the chocolate and butter into a bowl and melt over a pan of simmering water. As soon as it has melted, remove the bowl from the heat and cool slightly for a minute or so.

Put the egg yolks and sugar into a bowl and whisk with an electric beater until pale and creamy. Stir the cream and the rum, if using, into the melted chocolate mixture, then quickly fold in the egg yolk mixture. Put the egg whites into a clean bowl and whisk until soft peaks form. Quickly fold into the chocolate mixture.

Pour into the pastry case and bake for 25 minutes until risen and a bit wobbly. Remove from the oven and let cool – the filling will sink and firm up as it cools. Dust with confectioners' sugar, and serve at room temperature with cream.

Cardamom adds an exotic aftertaste to this satin-smooth chocolate tart. I wrote this recipe while staying in France. It was spring, and violets were peeping up along the drive to the house. I decided to crystallize them to decorate the tart for the photograph – and here they are – my *violettes de Toulouse*! Gold almond dragées would also look spectacular for a really special occasion!

chocolate and cardamom cream tart

1 recipe Just-Push-It-In Pastry (page 41) or Pâte Sucrée (page 26)

chocolate and cardamom filling

300 ml double cream

4 cardamom pods, crushed

250 g plain dark chocolate (minimum 60 per cent cocoa solids)

3 tablespoons caster sugar

to finish

300 ml double cream

a couple of pinches of ground cardamom

confectioners' sugar, to taste

crystallized violets, to decorate*

a tart tin, 20 cm diameter

foil and baking beans

serves 6

*Gather the violets in the morning when they are fresh. Dry them, then paint the petals with just foamy, beaten egg white. Dust with caster sugar and put onto a wire cake rack in a warm place to dry – at least overnight. They should completely dry out and become brittle and crisp. To store, pack between layers of kitchen paper in an airtight container.

If using Pâte Sucrée, bring to room temperature. Preheat the oven to 190°C (375°F) Gas 5.

Roll out the pastry thinly on a lightly floured work surface, then use to line the tart tin. Prick the base, then chill or freeze for 15 minutes. Line with foil and baking beans and bake blind for 15 minutes. Remove the foil and beans, turn the oven down to 180°C (350°F) Gas 4 and return to the oven for 10–15 minutes to dry out and brown. Cool and remove from the tin, then transfer to a serving platter.

If using Just-Push-It-In Pastry, line the tin with the pastry rounds. Chill or freeze for 15 minutes, then bake blind following the method given on page 19. Let cool, then remove from the tin and transfer to a serving platter.

Put the cream and cardamom pods into a saucepan and heat until almost boiling. Remove from the heat and set aside to infuse for 20 minutes. When the cream is infused, put the chocolate and sugar into a bowl set over a pan of simmering water. Strain the cream over the chocolate and stir occasionally until melted.

Remove from the heat and let cool. Watch it carefully – just as it begins to thicken and set, start whisking with a hand beater. Whisk for 5 minutes until thick and light, then pour into the pastry case. Let set.

To finish, whip the double cream and flavour with the ground cardamom and confectioners' sugar, to taste. Decorate the tart as you like, with the whipped cardamom cream and the crystallized violets.

This recipe comes from Carl, the chef who cooked for us in a chalet in Méribel, France, during a skiing holiday. He was a fabulous cook and a dream of a pastry chef – this is one of his specialities.

carl's chocolate pecan tart with coffee bean sauce

1 recipe Sweet Rich Shortcrust Pastry (page 14, see note) or Pâte Sucrée (page 26)

1 egg, beaten, to glaze

chocolate filling

120 g dark chocolate (at least 60 per cent cocoa solids)

50 g unsalted butter

3 large eggs, beaten

175 ml maple syrup

250 g pecan nuts

coffee bean sauce

1 vanilla pod, split lengthways

300 ml milk

1 tablespoon finely ground espresso coffee

1 tablespoon caster sugar

2 medium egg yolks

2 tablespoons Cognac or Armagnac

a tart tin, 23 cm diameter

foil and baking beans

serves 6

Bring the pastry to room temperature. Preheat the oven to 190°C (375°F) Gas 5.

If using Sweet Rich Shortcrust Pastry, roll out on a lightly floured work surface and use to line the tart tin. Prick the base and chill or freeze for 15 minutes. Bake blind following the method on page 19. Glaze with beaten egg and bake again for 5–10 minutes. Let cool.

If using Pâte Sucrée, bring to room temperature. Roll out the pastry thinly on a lightly floured work surface, then use to line the tart tin. Prick the base, then chill or freeze for 15 minutes. Line with foil and baking beans and bake blind for 15 minutes. Remove the foil and beans, turn the oven down to 180°C (350°F) Gas 4 and return to the oven for 10–15 minutes to dry out and brown. Glaze with the beaten egg and bake again for 5–10 minutes. Let cool.

To make the chocolate filling, lower the oven to 160°C (325°) Gas 3. Break up the chocolate and put it into the top of a double boiler or a bowl set over a simmering pan of water. Add the butter and stir over gentle heat until melted. Put the eggs and maple syrup into a bowl and beat well. Add to the the chocolate. Stir well, and keep stirring over a low heat until the mixture starts to thicken. Stir in the pecan nuts and pour into the pastry case.

Bake for 35–40 minutes until just set – the filling will still be a bit wobbly.

Meanwhile, to make the sauce, put the vanilla pod, milk, coffee and sugar into a saucepan and heat gently. Bring almost to the boil, then set aside to infuse for 15 minutes. Remove the vanilla pod.*

Put the egg yolks into a bowl, beat well, then pour in the infused milk. Mix well and return to the pan. Stir with a wooden spoon over gentle heat until the custard coats the back of the spoon. Pour into a cold bowl and stir in the Cognac. Cover with clingfilm, cool and chill until needed.

Serve the tart warm with the coffee bean sauce – or with cream.

*Note Rinse and dry the pod, and store in a sugar jar to make vanilla sugar.

My sister is responsible for this outrageous recipe. We were chatting about brownies one night and she came up with the idea of making a walnut crust for the tart instead of having the nuts in the filling. Here is the result. My niece Cassia helped to stir the mixture for the tart in the photograph – I wonder if there was any ulterior motive in her kind gesture?

double chocolate brownie tart with walnut crust

150 g digestive biscuits

150 g walnuts

125 g unsalted butter, melted

brownie filling

125 g dark plain chocolate, broken into small pieces

175 g butter

400 g caster sugar

3 large eggs, beaten

1 teaspoon real vanilla essence

150 g all-purpose flour

200 g white chocolate chips

a deep cake tin, 23 cm square

non-stick baking parchment

makes about 16 brownies

Line the base of the tin with a square of non-stick baking parchment to make removing the finished tart easier.

To make the base, crush the biscuits and walnuts in a food processor, pulsing to keep the biscuits and nuts quite coarse. Stir the biscuits into the melted butter until evenly coated. Press evenly into the base and 4 cm up the sides of the tin (a flat potato masher will help you to do this) before it cools. Chill in the refrigerator for 20 minutes to set the base before filling.

Preheat the oven to 180°C (350°F) Gas 4.

To make the filling, put the chocolate into a small bowl and melt over a pan of hot water. Put the butter and sugar into a bowl, cream until light and fluffy, then beat in the eggs. Stir in the melted chocolate and vanilla. Fold in the flour, then half the chocolate chips. Spoon into the biscuit case and level the top. Sprinkle with the remaining chocolate chips.

Bake for 35 minutes or until a cocktail stick inserted into the middle reveals fudgy crumbs. Do not overcook.

Cool in the tin. When cool, turn out of the tin and cut into 16 pieces.

This soft, sticky tart packed with walnuts is superb with the easy vanilla ice cream marbled with fudge toffee.

walnut tart

with quick fudge ice cream

1 recipe Sweet Rich Shortcrust Pastry
(page 14, see note)

walnut filling

125 g unsalted butter, softened

125 g light soft brown sugar

3 large eggs

grated zest and juice of 1 small orange

175 g golden syrup

225 g shelled walnut pieces

a pinch of salt

quick fudge ice cream

150 g chewy toffees (such as Werther's)

100 g double cream

1 tub (600 ml) best quality vanilla
ice cream, softened

a fluted tart tin, 23 cm diameter

serves 6

Bring the pastry to room temperature. Preheat the oven to 190°C (375°F) Gas 5.

Roll out the pastry on a lightly floured work surface and use to line the tart tin. Prick the base, chill or freeze for 15 minutes, then bake blind following the method given on page 19. Cool. Lower the oven to 180°C (350°F) Gas 4.

To make the filling, put the butter and sugar into a bowl and cream until light and fluffy. Gradually beat in the eggs, one at a time. Beat the orange zest and juice into the butter and egg mixture. Heat the golden syrup in a small saucepan until runny, but not very hot. Stir into the butter mixture, then stir in the walnuts and salt.

Pour into the pastry case and bake for 45 minutes until lightly browned and risen. The tart will sink a little on cooling.

While the tart is cooling, make the ice cream. Put the toffees and double cream into a small saucepan and stir over a medium heat to melt. Cool slightly and stir quickly into the ice cream so that it looks marbled. Put the ice cream back in the freezer until ready to serve.

Serve the tart at room temperature with scoops of the fudge ice cream.

A deliciously moist and almondy tart with a crust of caramelized pine nuts. This is perfect served with coffee or with fresh peaches and apricots.

frangipane pine nut tart

1 recipe Pâte Sucrée (page 26) or My Just-Push-It-In Pastry (page 41)

almond filling

100 g blanched almonds

100 g caster sugar

100 g unsalted butter, softened

5 large eggs, beaten

2 tablespoons Marsala or dark rum

a pinch of salt

100 g all-purpose flour

to finish

100 g pine nuts

2 tablespoons confectioners' sugar

a baking sheet

a loose-based tart tin, 25 cm diameter

serves 6

If using Pâte Sucrée, bring the pastry to room temperature. Preheat the oven to 200°C (400°F) Gas 6, then set the baking sheet on the middle shelf.

Roll out the pastry thinly on a lightly floured work surface, use to line the tart tin and prick the base all over. Alternatively, line the tin with My Just-Push-It-In Pastry rounds. Chill or freeze for 15 minutes.

To make the almond filling, put the almonds and sugar into a food processor and grind until the almonds are as fine as possible. Add the butter and blend until creamy. Gradually blend in the beaten eggs, then add the Marsala or rum and the pinch of salt. Finally, add the flour, blending quickly until just mixed.

Spread the filling over the base of the tart, then sprinkle with the pine nuts. Don't worry if there seems to be too little filling – it will rise.

Bake on the preheated baking sheet for about 10 minutes, until the pastry begins to brown at the edges, then lower the heat to 180°C (350°F) Gas 4 and bake for a further 20 minutes until puffed, brown and set.*

Remove the tart from the oven and turn up the heat to 230°C (450°F) Gas 8. Sift the confectioners' sugar over the top in a thin and even layer. Return to the oven for 5 minutes or less, until the sugar melts and caramelizes. (Alternatively, put under a preheated grill, protecting the pastry edges with foil, for a couple of minutes until the sugar caramelizes.) Serve warm.

*Note Because the tart is not baked blind, slipping it onto a preheated baking sheet will help to make the base cook quickly and crisply.

mail order and websites

The Cooks Kitchen
Tel: 0117 9070903 for catalogue.
Online mail order : www.kitchenware.co.uk
Mail order company with everything you could need for pastry-making and baking, including rolling pins, ceramic baking beans, best quality heavy duty tins and baking sheets. And lots more besides.

Wares of Knutsford
Household and Hardware Emporium
36a Princess St
Knutsford, Cheshire
Tel: 01565 751477.
Mail order at : www.waresofknutsford.co.uk Good old-fashioned quality ironmongers selling a selection of kitchen and bakeware including tins, lattice-maker, measuring jugs and measuring spoons.

Lakeland Limited
Alexandra Buildings
Windermere
Cumbria LA23 1BQ
Tel: 015394 88100
Fax: 015394 88300
www.lakelandlimited.com
Huge range of high quality bakeware and cookery equipment available by mail order, online and from their shops. Some hard-to-find ingredients also available. Fast and friendly service. Phone for a catalogue.

Nisbets
Freepost BS4675
Bristol BS2 0YZ
Tel: 0117 955583
www.nisbets.co.uk
A comprehensive guide to light catering equipment. Three editions of the catalogue are produced each year.

W.M. Page
121 Shaftesbury Avenue
London W1
Tel: 020 7379 6334
Excellent baking equipment.

Silverwood Limited
Ledsam Street Works
Birmingham B16 8DN
Tel: 0121 454 3571/2
Fax: 0121 454 6749
Email: Sales@AlanSilverwood.co.uk
Professional quality bread and cake tins and trays; bakeware which should last a lifetime. Aga range too. Stocked by Lakeland, John Lewis stores, major department stores and cook shops. For local stockists write or phone for details.

Divertimenti
139–141 Fulham Road
London SW3 6SD
Tel: 020 7581 8065
Fax: 020 7823 9429
33–34 Marylebone High Street
London W1U 4PT
Tel: 020 7935 0689
www.divertimenti.co.uk
Two shops in London plus mail order catalogue for a wide range of equipment. Knife sharpening and copper retinning service. On-line cooks' chatroom 'The Kitchen Table'.

David Mellor
4 Sloane Square
London SW1 8EE
Tel: 020 7730 4259
www.davidmellordesign.co.uk
Well-stocked shop plus mail order catalogue.

Leon Jaeggi & Sons
77 Shaftesbury Avenue
London W1V 7DJ
Tel: 020 7434 4545
www.d-
Professional catering equipment, open to the public.

index